FOLLOWING
JESUS
ON THE WAY

FOLLOWING JESUS ON THE WAY

Biblical Meditations on Lenten Themes

CHRISTOPHER DORN

EQUIP PRESS

FOLLOWING JESUS ON THE WAY

Copyright © 2020 Christopher Dorn

All rights reserved. No part of this publication may be reproduced, distributed, or transmitted in any form or by any means, without prior written permission.

Published by Equip Press, Colorado Springs, CO

Scripture quotations marked (NIV) are taken from the Holy Bible, New International Version. Copyright © 1973, 1978, 1984, 2011 by Biblica, Inc.® Used by permission. All rights reserved worldwide.

Scripture quotations marked (NRSV) are taken from the New Revised Standard Version Bible, copyright © 1989 the Division of Christian Education of the National Council of the Churches of Christ in the United States of America. Used by permission. All rights reserved.

First Edition: 2020
Following Jesus on the Way / Christopher Dorn
Paperback ISBN: 978-1-951304-42-3
eBook ISBN: 978-1-951304-43-0
Library of Congress Control Number: 2020922019

CONTENTS

Foreword 7
Introduction 13

FIRST SERIES

1. To Begin Again 17
2. An Unlikely Story 23
3. The Scandal of the Cross 29
4. Impatient on the Way 35
5. The Obedience of the Son 41
6. Fragile Possibilities, Robust Hopes 47

SECOND SERIES

7. To Doubt God's Goodness 53
8. In the Face of Opposition 59
9. The Severity and Kindness of God 65
10. Running 71
11. Justification by Faith 77
12. A Royal Welcome 83

THIRD SERIES

13. Need, Temptation, Obedience 89
14. Is There Hope Even for Me? 95
15. Search for Satisfaction 101
16. A Drama of Conversion 107
17. No More Tears 113
18. Subduing his Enemies 121

FOREWORD

Christopher Dorn's new Lenten series is a welcomed lift to flagging sprits struggling in hard times. He never loses sight of the mark, which is the difficult path we choose in Christ to make our way from the cross to the empty tomb. Three things make this series stand out.

First, Dorn keeps our eyes fixed on the assigned texts of the lectionary. Beginning with Chapter 1 in Year B (First Series), we immediately recognize his profound grasp of Old and New Testament detail. Even as he draws us into the texts, Dorn invites us to "pause now to see what God has to show us." And so, beyond ancient words on familiar pages, it is the symbols and their deeper meaning that come to life for us.

Second, Dorn provides personal and recognizable illustrations and anecdotes that entice us into the Lenten drama. For example, in Chapters 3 and 4 (First Series), we enter the desert of doubt. Here in the wilderness, we come to realize that postmodern misgivings about the Christian message are not really based on proven falsehoods as so many allege, but on a predisposition not to believe. Who, after all, claims victory in the face of the incredible horror of the cross? Rather, Lent's offering is a spiritual alternative reality. Unlike a debate over competing theories, the Lenten saga simply asks us to lay aside doubt and believe, and so find ourselves embedded in the story with Jesus.

Finally, this is Incarnational Christology at its best. The divine and human natures of Christ are intact, and Dorn's careful approach helps us to see the one person of Christ with no mixing of natures, no compromise that would allow us to lose sight either of his tremendous suffering or his complete confidence in his mission in reliance on the Holy Spirit. Thus, Dorn's Christology is aptly complemented by his Pneumatology.

As a result of the manner in which Dorn draws us into the saga, we find ourselves almost immediately adrift in the wilderness with Jesus, just as hungry, just as alone, just as vulnerable. We learn it is a chastening and tempering place, but also a place of holiness from time immemorial. The sights and sounds are indeed ancient, and yet at the same time, current. Just as the people of Israel contended with hunger and thirst in the desert, so also a young man with a new job in a strange and unfriendly city is alone and unhappy in his own desert. And so, we share a common reality with this young man, but also with our Lord. Together we must come to terms with the raw fact of sin and a broken world. To underestimate that reality is to render Lent meaningless.

Still, the answer to our crying out to God who listens in silence might surprise us. We are told that, even as we struggle to call out to God in our pain, he has already heard us, already acted for us, and already showed us mercy. The great high priest, Jesus the Christ, is now interceding for us. The one who in his life and death achieved what today we call "street cred" has been to the desert with all of its angst and violence, suffered its heat and thirst, and, by his obedience, undone what the devil and we, his accomplices, did.

As we make our way in the wilderness, we also discover, pardon the pun, a compelling dryness to Dorn's humor, as he bids us to get acquainted with the devil. It's important! Because only by so doing will we shed the devil of the trappings of popular imagination, and learn about the one who knows how much we desire forbidden fruit, and how much we desire success at any cost. Satan, the one who can turn even our idea of complete trust in God into a selfish desire to appear pious, is not to be trifled with. His scheme is subterfuge of the cleverest sort. He is even capable of counterstrategy. Failing to tempt Jesus twice before, he changes tactics, seeking to undermine our Lord's confidence in the goodness of God. But, in fact, it is not really a test of Jesus, as it might appear. Rather, it is an evil test of God. For Jesus to follow through on the devil's third temptation would be to redirect confidence from God to his own self-confidence and, by our association with him, confidence in ourselves. Jesus knew better. The rescue of God was by his providence and not by way of proving God's loyalty.

Especially powerful are the three Palm Sunday meditations. Here is where we see the contrast of the bitter peace of Rome, which was won by violence, and the peace of Christ, which was won by selfless service and sacrifice. With frequent visits to our time and place, we again find ourselves in the narrative. For us to discover the authentic peace of Christ, it is necessary to follow in his footsteps from the mountaintop to the Valley of the Shadow of Death. Dorn leads us down the mountain in suspense. But will we go willingly?

These Palm Sunday meditations are especially dramatic, as they should be. We become actors in the triumphal procession into Jerusalem, learning of our Old Testament roots along the route, and finding the real meaning of why we too would line the streets to shout "Hosanna!" We learn of the poverty driving the Jews' restless ambitions and extravagant hope of a deliverer. Are we so different? We recognize the crushed self-esteem of a proud people. And yet when in the world has the desire for self-esteem been greater?

Dorn challenges us to ponder this. The self-esteem on offer from the world is a fiction. We cannot find it where the poisoned promises of a tinsel-laced world would place it. Only when we recognize how much God, in love, esteems us, will we find the measure of self-esteem necessary for peace of mind.

But can God really be trusted? We live in a world that distrusts God or dismisses him entirely. The age-old problem of theodicy looms large today. Chapter 9 in Year C (Second Series) begins with this dilemma, and we learn how Jesus, with his amazing parables and saving miracles, was initially successful in his ministry. But the world is fickle, and as his ministry comes under attack, we struggle to find a clear answer to where God is in all of this. Had Jesus been abandoned or was he deceived from the beginning? We are not given help with our questions of God's reality.

Instead, we are provided a reliable picture of the Father. It is a picture of his equal measure of justice and mercy. The Father is bent on justice, but the time of mercy has been extended and proclaimed by the Son whose time is short. The message is clear: "Don't delay!" And so, we are treated by Dorn to a rich eschatology, one that does not so much answer the question of theodicy as it defangs the question by reminding us of our place at the banquet table with its glimpses of the new heaven and new earth.

Finally, I want to draw the readers' attention to a wonderful treatment of the story of the Prodigal Son found in Chapter 10 in Year C (Second Series). This universally loved parable typically has interpreters focusing on the prodigal or, more importantly, the gracious father. Dorn has provided us with a sympathetic understanding of all the characters in the story, especially the way they relate to each other. This complex of relationships feels lifelike and it reminds us again that, while so much has changed, so much has remained the same.

FOREWORD

So, with the same urgency Jesus expressed when he bid us not to delay, I would ask you not to hesitate to treat yourself and those to whom you minister to this wonderful Lenten series. It will provide three richly rewarding years of Lenten insight.

— Reverend Dr. Linden DeBie
The Colonial Church of Bayside, Queens
Reformed Church in America

INTRODUCTION

Lent is a season of preparation for the celebration of Easter. For many Christians, it is an occasion for renewed devotion to Jesus, for a recommitment to follow him on the way to the cross—and through the cross to the empty tomb. For good reason, then, the season begins on a day dedicated to themes of repentance, prayer, and spiritual disciplines. We refer here to Ash Wednesday, when we hear the call to repentance and receive on our foreheads the imposition of ashes, a visible mark of this call to us in our solidarity with a sinful humanity destined for death. "From dust you came, to dust you shall return. Repent, therefore, and believe the gospel!"

From Ash Wednesday, the season unfolds over the next forty days, excluding the Sundays contained within it. (Since Sundays are always "feast" days, during which we celebrate the resurrection of Jesus from the dead regardless of the period in the church calendar, they are not counted in a season marked by repentance and spiritual disciplines.) It is apt, then, that we encounter the Latin ordinal number "Quadragesima" (fortieth) already on the first Sunday in Lent, which in earlier times was known as "Quadragesima Sunday." It is a curious convention, however, considering the fact that this Sunday is not the fortieth day, but instead marks a period that is to extend forty days.

Why forty days? The period of forty is significant in both the Old and New Testaments of the Bible. During the days of Noah, rain falls upon the earth forty days and nights, wiping out every living thing

(Gen. 7:4). Moses spends forty years in the desert of Midian in exile after killing the Egyptian (Acts 7:30). The children of Israel wander in the desert forty years before entering into the Promised Land (Num. 14:33; 32:13; Deut. 2:7). Moses is on top of Mount Sinai for forty days before coming down with the two tablets of God's law (Ex. 24:18). Strengthened by food provided by an angel, the prophet Elijah travels forty days and nights until he reaches Horeb, the mountain of God (1 Kings 19:8). To the inhabitants of the city of Nineveh the prophet Jonah preaches: "Forty days and Nineveh will be destroyed," prompting them to fast and repent in sackcloth and ashes (Jon. 3:4). Jesus fasts for forty days in the desert, where he is tempted by Satan, before launching his public ministry (Matt. 4:2; Mark 1:13; Luke 4:2).

These texts, among others, can be seen to contain many of the themes that find expression during the season of Lent. Throughout the forty days, God's people are invited to watch and to wait, to fast and to pray, to repent and to "make level paths for their feet" (Heb. 12:13). All this is meant for the testing and proving of their faith with the aim of spiritual renewal, associated with the Easter Triduum (or the "Great Three Days"). It is in these three days, which include Good Friday, Holy Saturday, and Easter Sunday, that the Lenten season dramatically culminates, as we have already indicated.

The meditations compiled in this book explore these, as well as other themes, in conjunction with each of the six Sundays in Lent. They are based on texts designated for those Sundays as drawn from the Revised Common Lectionary, a three-year cycle of Bible readings used by churches of various denominations and confessional traditions on the occasion of Sunday worship. The three years that comprise this cycle are designated A, B, and C. Because the date of their publication (2021) coincides with Year B, the meditations based on this year's readings appear first in the series, followed by C and A. This choice of arrangement is dictated by my wish to place into the hands of pastors, worship committees, and lectionary study groups a ready resource to be used in preparation for the current Lenten season. This, of course, is not to exclude individuals, for whom these meditations can serve as a means by which to engage one of the more important Lenten spiritual disciplines, that of prayerful study and reflection. For this purpose, I recommend finding a quiet place, lighting a candle, and reading one meditation per session. Note what thoughts and questions arise. Perhaps afterward, take a few moments just to listen. Then conclude the session with prayer.

My sincere hope is that all those who read these meditations may emerge from the time they spend in them with the sense that they have entered more profoundly and meaningfully into the spirit of the Lenten season as a result. Inspired by this spirit, may we all come to a renewed appreciation of what it means to follow Jesus on the way.

TO BEGIN AGAIN

MARK 1:9-15

The gospel lesson designated for this Lord's Day represents an abrupt shift. On Transfiguration Sunday we were with Jesus and Moses and Elijah on the summit of a mountain, where Jesus appeared in the resplendent glory that he shares with God, because he is God's own beloved Son (Mark 9:2-9). However, we realized that we could not remain on the majestic heights, but had to accompany Jesus and his disciples down the mountain. We can already anticipate what this means. Indeed, we use the phrase figuratively in our own language. When it is said of someone that he has come down from the mountain, we know that he has returned from a peak experience. Whatever it was that he found exhilarating has passed, and he must return to the face the ordinary and routine, or even the difficult and the challenging.

From the mountain, then, we have come down, and we are now in the desert. This is the place where our Lenten journey begins. Just as Jesus was forty days in the wilderness, so must we begin here with him in the forty days preceding Easter. Here there is a need to develop a competence in interpreting biblical symbols. Just as the mountain is a symbol rich with meanings in the Bible, as we found in the scene of Jesus' transfiguration, so also is the desert. The desert symbolizes chaos, danger, temptation, sin, and death. This immediately gives rise to the question: "If Jesus is God's own beloved Son, how can God expose him to the life-negating forces of the desert?" That does not seem to be at all compatible with love. That it's God's will that Jesus go into the desert, however, Mark wants to make very clear. He tells us explicitly that the Spirit drives him out into the desert. This is a deep mystery, and Lent is the time to contemplate such a mystery. God does not drive Jesus into the desert to be swallowed up there, but to succeed in the place where Israel before him failed. In this connection, we should see in the number "40" a reference to the forty years that Israel wandered in the desert. "Remember how the Lord led you all the way in the desert these forty years, to humble and test you, in order to know what was in your hearts," Moses exhorts the Israelites (Deut. 8:2). We know that Israel did not pass this test; the people revolted against God, and their bodies fell in the desert. But for Jesus, the outcome is very different. In finding contemporary language to explain this contrast, we may say that in Jesus Christ, God gives Israel, and by extension, all humankind a "reset." In exposing himself to the life-negating forces of the desert, Jesus overcomes them for us. And in overcoming them, he transforms them. By God's grace, they now become for us conditions for growth and renewal, for change and new beginnings in him. Let us then in the next few moments meditate on the desert in this perspective. Let us first see it as a place for clarifying our vision; then, let us consider it as a place for preparing for a new role; and, finally, let us view it as place for developing intimacy with God.

The desert is a solitary place. Perhaps this is the first image that our mind conjures up when we hear the word. Here we are very much alone. Free from the noise of distractions and the presence of others, we have only our own thoughts to keep us company. Many in our world avoid this experience at all costs, because they cannot bear to be alone with themselves. After all, it is in the dry and arid places, according to Jesus in Matthew's Gospel, that demons wander (12:43). And it is very often in the solitude of the desert that one has to wrestle with his demons. Does not Jesus himself know this experience? Should we not interpret Mark's words in this regard? We read that Jesus was in the desert, tempted by Satan. We have already seen that Jesus does not shun the solitude of the desert; rather, he exposes himself to it. For this reason, we do not need to fear it, provided that we are in him and with him. From the experience can come something positive for us, even if it is painful. The solitude heightens our awareness; it sharpens our spiritual perception. As we wait on God, we come to see our life, our life's course, with greater clarity. In this sense, then, the desert becomes a place for clarifying our vision.

This outcome of our time in the desert is often associated with what are going to be discussing next. We refer here to the desert as a place for preparing for a new role. Let me hasten to add that this does not have to mean a change in life circumstances. A new role can also mean a recommitment to an existing one, which is also an important Lenten discipline. In any case, this is difficult, because it means change. Our experience in the desert will induce change when we undergo it. We've already mentioned that the desert is a symbol of chaos. In his book, *12 Rules for Life*, Jordan Peterson defines chaos as "unexplored territory." Chaos extends, without limit, beyond all states, all ideas, and all disciplines, according to Peterson. All this is to say that chaos is the unfamiliar. In the desert, we are without signposts, without a map, without a set of reference points. Is this not what it means to wander in our deserts? To wander means to be without a destination. This is not a pleasant experience, but a painful one. People who wander without a perceived destination become fearful and anxious, and when the anxiety becomes too great, they panic. They begin to pine for the old and the familiar, even when it no longer holds promise for their lives.

Again, consider the people of Israel. Moses has brought them to the edge of the desert. Before them is the promised land. A delegation of leading men is sent to spy out the land. The spies bring back a report that reduces the people to terror and tears. They cry out, "Would it not be better for us to return to Egypt? ... Let us appoint a leader and return to Egypt!" (Num. 14:3, 4). Egypt is a place of bondage and misery, but at least it's familiar. The story of the people of Israel wandering in the desert illustrates a great tragedy of human life. We prefer bondage and misery to the unfamiliar. We forfeit the growth and the new beginnings that come from the willingness to move out into unexplored territory. If we've lived long enough, we know this to be true because we too have failed here, maybe even miserably. Maybe some of us have lingering regrets here, because we can see in retrospect how things might have turned out otherwise for us if we had risen to the challenges at those critical junctures of our lives. We have already mentioned that in Jesus Christ this failure does not have to have the last word. We've already said that Jesus succeeds where Israel, where we, failed. When Jesus emerges from the desert, he assumes his new role as bearer of God's kingdom and begins his public ministry. For our part, as a youth pastor once told me, God is faithful in that God will keep us in our desert until he accomplishes the change in us that he intends. This means that the chaos of our deserts can still serve as the condition for our growth and renewal despite our past failures.

Let us then move to our third and final observation. Here we have to explain what we mean when we say that the desert is a place for developing intimacy with God. Already we should see that this process is implicit in the first two things. Clarifying our vision depends on waiting on God to reveal his will for our lives. "Make known to me your ways, O Lord; teach me your paths. Lead me in your truth, and teach me; for I wait on you all day long," we say in verses 4 and 5 of Psalm 25 (NRSV), which is appointed for this first Sunday of Lent.

And preparing for a new role involves trusting God as he leads us into unexplored territory. Of course, both mean growing in intimacy with God. All this is true; however, the desert itself appears to be a special place for love between God and God's people. "When Israel was a child, how I loved him, and out of Egypt I called my son," God avows (Hos. 11:1). God speaks wistfully of the time that he subsequently spent in the desert with the people of Israel: "I remember the devotion of your youth, how as a bride you loved me, and followed me through the desert," as we read in the prophet Jeremiah (2:2). "Therefore, I am now going to allure her; I will lead her into the desert and speak tenderly to her," says the Lord through the prophet Hosea (2:14). No less is this love experienced by Jesus, God's own beloved Son. We read that Jesus was in the desert, and the angels attended him. Angels in the Bible always mean that the barrier between heaven and earth has been breached. The presence of angels gives us evidence that the divine and human realms have interpenetrated. You will remember Jacob's ladder, on which Jacob saw angels ascending and descending. He was compelled to exclaim that this is none other than the house of God and the gate of heaven (Gen. 28:17). Remember that Jesus told Nathanael his disciple that he, Jesus himself, is the site where angels ascend and descend (John 1:51). In him the barrier between heaven and earth has been decisively breached. He is the gate of heaven. In and with Jesus in the desert, we know intimacy with God.

With intimacy with God comes inner peace and harmony, of which we have an image in our lesson. We read that he was in the desert and was with the wild beasts. Our first thought is to associate the wild beasts with the life-negating forces of the desert. Many commentators see in this detail a reference to Isaiah's vision of the messianic age when "the wolf will live with the lamb, the leopard will lie down with the goat, the calf and the lion and the yearling together. And the lion will eat straw like the ox" (Isa. 11: 6-7). Jesus is the promised Messiah who will bring this new age. This is the hope of the people of God then and now. In the final analysis, the presence of Jesus in the desert points to a bright future: God will bring harmony out of discord, peace out of strife, and order out of chaos. No doubt this is at the heart of the good news of God that Jesus comes out of the desert to proclaim. But it seems that it is not possible for us to appreciate this good news until we go into the desert with Jesus. So let us go then to meet Jesus in the desert. Let us begin our Lenten journey of forty days there. Amen.

2

AN UNLIKELY STORY

MARK 8:31-38; ROMANS 4:13-25

"Then he began to teach them that the Son of Man must suffer many things, and be rejected by the elders and chief priests and the scribes and be killed, and after three days rise again." This first verse of the gospel lesson designated for this Sunday is difficult for us to hear, especially after the consolation we received in the desert last time. We learned that the desert is a special place of love between God and God's people, a place that God remembers wistfully because God and Israel enjoyed an intimacy there before their relationship would later become strained to the breaking point. We also caught a glimpse of the peace and harmony that will exist among all God's creatures in the messianic age when we noted that Jesus was with the wild beasts there. Nor did we neglect to mention that Jesus emerged from the desert in the power of his prophetic office, preaching the good news of God's kingdom. During the Sundays in Epiphany, we saw that with a word, he drove out demons. With a touch, he healed people of their illnesses. He was even transfigured in his appearance on the mountain heights, clothed in the resplendent glory that he shares with God because he is God's own beloved Son. Today the strife and violence that Jesus predicts is awaiting him clashes with everything that we have seen so far. To use a metaphor that will resonate with musicians, these are dissonant notes in the melody of Jesus' life that we have not heard until now.

Today our lesson invites us to identify with Peter. That is to say, we are to imagine that we are an eyewitness of all these things. Then we are to imagine not only that we are present with the one who wields this power but are also his closest ally and confidant. How could fortune have favored us more? How could we have hitched our wagon to a brighter star? We walk tall. Our face is always beaming. Then the unthinkable happens. Who we thought this one was turns out to be quite unlike the image we formed of him. He begins to speak of something regarding himself that contradicts our image of him. A chasm between what is real and what we imagined as real opens up. In our anxiety, we protest: "This cannot be! This is not who you are! These things will never happen to you!" Parenthetically, it is important to mention that moments before, Peter made a proper identification of Jesus. When Jesus asked his disciples, "Who do you say that I am?" Peter was the first to volunteer an answer: "You are the Messiah" (Mark 8:29). Now Peter, the gifted theologian, is the one who does not have divine things in mind, but mere human things. Now Peter, the closest ally and confidant of Jesus, is Satan who stands opposed to Jesus and to God's plan.

If we're beginning to sense that the scene portrayed in our lesson is meant to challenge assumptions and overturn expectations about Jesus, then our instincts are sound. Indeed, if we do not see what is happening from this perspective, then we will certainly miss what it has to teach us. In looking carefully at this exchange between Jesus, on one hand, and Peter, the rest of the disciples, and the crowds, on the other, at least two questions emerge. First, what exactly is Jesus demanding of his disciples and the crowds if they want to be his disciples? Second, what does this exchange tell us about God?

Let me begin with an illustration. In his retirement years, Frank volunteered at a bicycle repair shop. There he befriended a man named Jeremy who helped him two afternoons a week. They talked about everything, and occasionally the subject of faith came up. Jeremy was a retired NASA space engineer and very rational in his approach to things. With his sharp mind trained to think scientifically, he analyzed the subject and concluded that atheism is the only credible option. Among the reasons he gave for rejecting faith is that it represents an escape from reality. To Jeremy, Christians are those who leap into a fantasy world because this world is too unbearable for them. People should resist this flight into fantasy and face the world on its own terms.

I'm sure it would surprise Jeremy to learn that what Jesus is telling the disciples and the crowds is something very similar. We hear him say: "Do you want to follow me? Let me bring you down from the clouds. I will be rejected and killed. If you follow me, you will have to go into it with both eyes open and accept what I am telling you without self-deception. Indeed, you will even have to take up your own cross."

It is significant that the word "cross" appears here in Mark for the first time. In first-century Rome, the cross was an instrument of torture and execution reserved for the basest of criminals. The contrast between the power and reputation of Jesus and the shame and degradation of a crucified criminal could not be starker. Here we can understand Peter's reaction. In any event, those who heard Jesus knew exactly that "cross" meant death. It meant losing one's life.

The Apostle Paul speaks of the scandal of the cross. Scandal in this sense refers to that which offends. Peter was right to see himself as a success as a disciple of Jesus. We want to be successful. We know intuitively that to be successful we have to associate with successful people. For example, this concept is the key to success in dating and romance: if we want to be successful at attracting and dating a potential mate, we need to shadow those who are already successful. When mentors and friends no longer prove they can meet our criterion for success, we tend to dissociate from them. We look for new mentors and friends. We have to believe that many who heard the words of Jesus that day were offended. Those who had considered following Jesus out of a desire for success began to look elsewhere. These words still offend today. There are very few who would say that in them is found a formula for success.

How then *are* we to understand what Jesus is demanding? Again, in his *12 Rules for Life*, Peterson tells us that we have a responsibility to see what is before our eyes, courageously, and to learn from it, even if it seems repugnant or even horrifying to us. The act of seeing is particularly important when it challenges what we know and what we rely on, upsetting and destabilizing us. This is the moment when we tend to retreat, when we willfully refuse to see what is there before us. Why? Because it means we have to change how we see things, which is painful. We prefer the comfort of our illusions to the truth about things as they really are. However, the truth is out there. That is why, according to Peterson, you are by no means what you already know. You are also all that which you *could* know, if only you *would*. For this reason, you should never sacrifice what you *could* be for what you already *are*. You should never give up the *better* that lies ahead for the *security* you already have—and certainly not when you have already caught a glimpse, an undeniable glimpse, of that which lies beyond.

So far as I know, Peterson is not a Christian in the strict sense of the word, but what he is saying is very much in the same spirit as that in which Jesus is teaching here. Only Jesus in effect reverses these statements and expresses them positively: "You *should* sacrifice what you already are for what you *could* be. You *should* give up the security you already have for the *better* that lies ahead." This is what his summons to deny oneself and take up the cross and follow him means. This is what he means when he states that those who want to save their life will lose it, but those who lose their life for his sake and for the sake of the gospel will save it.

We say of someone, "He is searching for a cause larger than himself" and we accept this as a basic human impulse. We know that an individual without connections, without involvements, shrivels up and dies inside. The individual who participates in a cause larger than himself thrives, provided it is a worthy cause. He has "lost" himself in the cause and lives his life for its sake. This means that he has oriented his own interests and values around the cause, which gives unity and direction, joy and meaning, to his life. In this light, does not the hard demand of Jesus turn out to be good news? It transforms religion from a burdensome list of "dos" and "don'ts" into spiritual adventure. Sadly, this is missed by those who contemptuously condemn the Christian faith as a slave morality. It is ignored by those in our culture who dismiss it as holding nothing of value for a meaningful life.

This brings us to our second question. We asked what this exchange between Jesus and his disciples tells us about God. When we encounter Jesus Christ, we begin to undergo a process by which we unlearn all that we knew about God, just as Peter did. God interacts with us and our world in ways that neither Peter nor we consider fitting for God. God takes our frail and finite humanity as he finds it and works from within it. Ultimately, our humanity has no special potential inherent in it; it is destined for death. This applies no less to the humanity of Jesus Christ himself. We have seen that this was a hard pill for Peter to swallow, especially after all that he had witnessed. In this there is no distinction between the strong and the weak, the rich and the poor, the young and old, the winner and the loser. Death is no respecter of persons. How is this good news?

Our epistle lesson gives us some guidance here. We learned about Abraham. What the Apostle Paul singles out for emphasis with respect to Abraham is God's promise to him. God promises to Abraham a son in his old age. But his wife Sarah is past her childbearing years. Nonetheless, the promise is that through this son, Abraham would become the father of many nations. Abraham faced the fact that his body was as good as dead, and that his wife's womb was barren. He did not waver in unbelief regarding God's promise, but was strengthened in his faith. For the God in whom he placed his faith is the God who gives life to the dead and calls into existence the things that do not exist (Rom. 4:17).

Abraham's God showed himself to be this God in Jesus Christ. We refer here to the mystery of Easter that still lies before us. With Peter we tend to hear in Jesus' statement only the parts about his suffering, rejection, and death. But Jesus also said that after three days he would rise again. It is always within the horizon of Easter that we courageously face the world on its own terms, taking up our cross to follow Jesus. Let us then continue moving forward in our Lenten journey in expectation that after the cross follows resurrection. Amen.

THE SCANDAL OF THE CROSS
1 CORINTHIANS 1:18-25; JOHN 2:13-22

Last time we learned that Jesus is going to be rejected by the elders and chief priests, be killed, and in three days rise again. We noted Peter's reaction, which served as an occasion for Jesus to make clear what it means to be a disciple. One must deny oneself, take up one's cross, and follow Jesus. We noted further that the word "cross" appears for the first time in Mark's Gospel in this context. To be Jesus' disciple means to bear a cross. This most certainly must have only scandalized the addressees of Jesus' words. What appeal is there in a cross? After all, one presumably decides to follow Jesus only when one determines that to do so will bring success. The cross, however, is a symbol of a failed life. How far removed is our conception of success from a cross!

In the epistle lesson designated for this Lord's Day, we see that the Apostle Paul also knows of the scandal of the cross. He tells us explicitly that not only is it a scandal to the Jews but also foolishness to the Gentiles. Obviously those who find in the message of the crucified Christ either scandal or foolishness are bound to reject it. But to those who accept it, it is the power of God and the wisdom of God. The Apostle Paul's observations here invite us to meditate on the message of the cross by means of these contrasting pairs of terms. Let us accordingly devote the next few moments to a close consideration of their meaning. First, we will ask why this message is perceived as "scandal" or "foolishness" by those who reject it. Afterward, we will proceed to determine the sense in which it is the "wisdom" and "power" of God for those who embrace it.

It is important to clarify at the outset that the word "scandal" in our lesson should be understood as "offense." The word "scandal" in our minds conjures up the image of a famous or widely admired person caught in a shameful or morally reprehensible act. We say that we are scandalized by this person's behavior. But this sense does not apply to the reaction of the Jews in Paul's day to his message of Christ crucified. Christ is the Greek word for "Messiah." The Messiah embodied the hope of the Jews, the hope of final triumph over their enemies and the establishment of a universal reign of justice and peace. The identification of such a figure with a homeless itinerant teacher executed by a method of torture reserved for slaves, insurrectionists, brigands, and pirates—that identification would have struck the Jews as offensive, as an affront to their dignity.

Why an affront to their dignity? Last time we observed that those with whom we are closely associated determine to a large extent our own status. If our social superiors are successful, then we tend to be seen as successful, and therefore have good reason to expect to share in their success, if we don't already. Conversely, when they no longer model success for us or even go so far as to prove themselves to be abject failures, then we dissociate from them. We recoil from the threat that we too will be branded as failures and so we shun their company. Our friends and family members may even warn us, if we are tempted to reconsider, that to continue to associate with them would be to commit "social suicide."

The sign above Jesus' cross read: "Jesus of Nazareth, the King of the Jews" (John 19:19). It can be read as the judgment on the part of the powerful and successful of the one whom they regarded as an impostor and therefore unworthy to be numbered among their ranks. It can also be read as a judgment of the Jews, as whose head and representative the sign identified Jesus. No closer association can exist than that between a king and his people. In the image of this failed Messiah, then, the Jews to whom Paul is preaching Christ crucified can only contemplate themselves as failures. In this perspective, how can they perceive the message of the cross of Christ as anything other than an affront to their dignity?

For his part, Paul does not deny or evade this association with the failure symbolized by the cross. He confides to the people at Corinth that it seems to him that "God put us apostles on display at the end of the procession, like those condemned to die in the arena" (1 Cor. 4:9). Indeed, he has become the "scum of the earth, the garbage of the world" (1 Cor. 4:13). He preaches Christ crucified because and as he has been crucified with Christ, so that it is no longer he who lives, but Christ who lives in him (Gal. 2:20). That is, he bears in his own body the death of Christ so that the life of Christ may also be revealed in his body (2 Cor. 4:11). This is for the benefit of those who accept his message, because as death is at work in him, life is at work in them (2 Cor. 4:12). Paul finds that he has this treasure in a vessel of clay (his mortal body), so that it is made clear that its power comes not from himself, but from God (2 Cor. 4:7).

About this power we will have more to say at the end our meditation; for now, let us proceed to ask how the message of the cross is foolishness to the Gentiles.

Here we may recall Paul's visit to Athens, which Luke recounts in his Acts of the Apostles (17:16-34). Paul talked with the people in the marketplace and the synagogue about Jesus Christ. This led them to invite him to the Areopagus, the site in Athens where the leading citizens deliberated on affairs vital to the life of the city. Among them were the intellectual elite of the day, whom Luke identifies as Stoic and Epicurean philosophers. After demonstrating his familiarity with their thought world, Paul elaborated his message about Jesus Christ, having added the claim that God appointed this one to be judge of all nations. This God proved by raising him from the dead. On hearing the message of the crucified and risen Christ, many scoffed, and Paul left the assembly.

To dismiss this message as foolishness is a reaction evident everywhere around us today. In this connection, let us recall Jeremy, the retired NASA engineer, whom we mentioned in the preceding meditation. For Jeremy, any intelligent man or woman ought to reject the message of the cross because religious faith is morally dishonest. Jeremy believes that we should learn to cope with life on its own terms, without taking refuge in comforting myths when life becomes too intolerable for us. Faith is a form of escapism, which is, at best, an immature response to the hardships of life.

Then there is the common misperception that Christian faith is incompatible with modern science. The experience of a young man named Mike is typical. Mike's passion for science in college led him to question and ultimately abandon the faith. "I just stopped believing in those Christian stories."

"Jews demand signs and Gentiles look for wisdom" (1 Cor. 1:22). But one wonders whether the Jews and the Gentiles here are self-deceived, whether the object of the demand or search is really the point. Could there have been a sign that settled once and for all that Jesus is the Christ? In the Gospel of John, the Jewish authorities are portrayed as the implacable enemies of Jesus. They are opposed to Jesus, refuse to believe in him, and always misunderstand him. These are the same men in whose presence Jesus performs many signs, but who, ironically, are always asking him to perform a sign to validate the claim he is making for himself. Could the presentation of Christ in philosophical concepts clothed in fine-sounding rhetoric really have convinced the wise man and the scholar of Paul's day? Or can a learned and systematic account of the Christian faith, especially one that addresses the kind of objections that Jeremy and Mike raise, ever really succeed in winning the intelligent and educated to the faith today? Have not all these individuals already decided in advance against faith? Have they not already adopted a disposition of mind that selects for what they will count as evidence for and against faith? "For since in the wisdom of God the world through its wisdom did not know him, God was pleased through the foolishness of what was preached to save those who believe" (1 Cor. 1:21). It is in the proclamation of the cross that God has chosen to encounter men and women, whether Jew or Gentile, strong or weak, rich or poor, young or old, winner or loser. For God is no "respecter of persons" (Acts 10:34).

Let us now shift our focus from those who reject the message to those who accept it. Let us ask first how it is the wisdom of God for the latter. We do not have the space here to give a comprehensive answer; let it suffice to say that the wisdom of God as revealed in the cross consists in its profound diagnosis of the human condition. The cross gives the starkest evidence that there exists in each of us forces that conspire together to plot our own destruction. Projects of self-improvement or community renewal or political reform generally yield only marginal results because they cannot get to the root of our problem. These forces have to be neutralized if we are to be healed, if we are to know peace with God and with one another. This is what has happened in the cross of Christ. It is there that that which drives us to destruction has been destroyed and removed from the driver's seat. This is what Paul recognizes and declares in his Letter to the Romans: "For God has done what the law, weakened by the flesh, could not do: by sending his own Son in the likeness of sinful flesh, and to deal with sin, he condemned sin in the flesh" (Rom. 8:3). In his *Radical Sacrifice*, the essayist Terry Eagleton writes that the crucifixion of Jesus Christ is "homeopathic medicine" that God administers to violent human beings to radically cure them.

This already reveals the power of the cross. For this reason, Paul can declare that he is not ashamed of it, because it brings salvation to all who believe, first to the Jew and then to the Gentile (Rom. 1:16). The cross demonstrates the power of God because in voluntarily submitting to it, Jesus resists and overcomes the world. No one can take his life from him; rather, he has the power to lay it down and take it up again on the command of his Father (John 10:18). Is this not what he declares in his confrontation with the Jews in our gospel lesson? There they demand to know by what authority he drives out the money changers from the temple. His reply is: "Destroy this temple and in three days I will raise it up" (John 2:19).

Paul proclaims Christ crucified. But the Christ who has been crucified is the same Christ who has been raised from the dead. Our gospel keeps before us the promise of Easter towards which we move in our Lenten journey together. Amen.

4

IMPATIENT ON THE WAY

NUMBERS 21:4-9; JOHN 3:14-21

The Old Testament lesson designated for this Lord's Day invites us to return to the desert. Since we are in the season of Lent, it is appropriate for us to be here, because we are still on our way to our destination in Easter. Today we are with the people of Israel, whom God has been faithfully leading through the desert. They have known his care and guidance. When they were thirsty and in need of water, he caused water to flow from the rock. When they were hungry and in need of food, he gave them manna, which he spread like a blanket on the desert floor each morning. The journey through the desert has become arduous, and the people have grown restive. In short, they have become impatient on the way. They complain against God and against Moses, and thereby bring swift disaster upon themselves. God sends among them fiery serpents, which bite and kill many of them. In their distress, they ask Moses to intercede with God, which Moses does. God then instructs Moses to make a bronze snake and place it on the top of a pole. If anyone who is bit looks at it, he lives.

This strange episode in the history of Israel contains a number of valuable lessons for us as we move deeper into the desert on our Lenten journey together. To benefit from them, we will have to reflect on Israel's experience with a view to what it can open up and reveal to us about our own. To this end, I propose that we organize our reflections by subordinating them under three points. The first we will call the tedium of the way; the second we will name the pain of frustration; and the third and final one, the sting of death.

The philosopher Friedrich Nietzsche tells us that he who has a "why" can bear any "how." That seems to me to be true, but only to a point. We can indeed bear difficult circumstances if we can see an end to them. "This too shall pass," as the saying goes. But when there is no end in sight, it is easy to feel impatient. If an end was at one time within reach, but has now receded from view, and we feel we are no longer making progress towards our goal, we grow even more impatient. The ancient Jewish sages tell us that this is the situation in which the nation of Israel finds itself here. The people said, "We were so close to entering the Promised Land, and now we are turning back. So did our fathers turn back and remain for thirty-eight years, until today." Do we know what it is like to be in this situation? We observed earlier that a characteristic of the desert is the absence of landmarks or signposts. That is to say, the desert lacks anything by which to chart our progress toward our goal. We prefer to have something tangible, something visible. God gives to his people his word, which contains a promise. It is not for us to know when God will fulfill his promise; it is only for us to trust in God's word, even and especially when our situation suggests that God has abandoned us in the desert, that God no longer seems concerned to bring us to the good place for which we at one time hoped in him.

Can God really be trusted? That it occurs to us to ask this question reflects at least our impatience in the desert. We have to understand the situation of Israel in this perspective. The people became "impatient." The translator's choice of this word is certainly legitimate with regard to Israel's situation, as we have seen, but the word renders a phrase that literally means "shortness or smallness of spirit." It really points to the incapacity on the part of the people to bear a load that is too big, too heavy. It is intolerable to them. They are overwhelmed by their trouble, because there is no place large enough in their hearts for their distress to settle, as the great Jewish sage Rashi rather poetically expresses it. Thus "impatient *on* the way" is at the same time "disheartened or discouraged *because* of the way."

With this observation, we have arrived at our second point. Impatience can yield to frustration, and frustration to real pain. Now it is clear that one of two options lie before God's people in their pain: Either they can rail against God for the putatively cruel treatment they have received at his hands or they can cry out to God in expectation that he will hear and save them. Both of these options are present in our lesson. One is the way of death and the other the way of life. But before we consider them, let us again admit that life in the desert can be harsh. The desert is a place of deprivation, a place of scarcity of resources. It seems to us our vital needs are unlikely to be met there. A young man told about his first real job after college. It was in a city hundreds of miles from where he grew up. However, the excitement of that first big move quickly faded. He had a small apartment with no furniture. He didn't know the city, or anyone in it. The job was interesting, but the loneliness was crushing. He was in his own desert, and it provoked a crisis in his faith.

"There is no bread! There is no water!" the people of Israel cry out in their frustration (Num. 21:5). To be sure, there is a grudging acknowledgement of God's provision. The miserable food they detest is a reference to the manna, by which God has been faithfully providing for their needs. But the manna is not at their disposal; they cannot hoard or accumulate it but must trust God to provide it anew each day. To be in this position of dependence on God in the desert is what made the food miserable to them. For deep in our sinful hearts is the demand to be the source of our own vital needs. The all-sufficient self is the dream of the sinful heart that turns into its nightmare. The deliverance from death that we need is at the same time deliverance from the prison of the all-sufficient self, which is incapable of giving and receiving love.

The tedium of our way combined with the pain of our frustration makes us vulnerable to temptation. Recall the two options we mentioned a few moments ago. To choose the first is to have already yielded to temptation. We have heard Israel's protest before: "You have brought us into this desert to destroy us; you do not really have our good at heart." When we have spoken in this way against God, it is a sign that we really have believed the oldest lie—the lie of the serpent in the Garden of Eden. That this is exactly what has happened in our lesson is confirmed by the appearance of the fiery serpents. No doubt this image is meant to point us to the serpent in the garden that tempted Adam and Eve to doubt God's goodness. If the fruit from the tree of the knowledge of good and evil is desirable, if it communicates qualities that God himself has, then why would God withhold it? If God is withholding from us what is for our good, then how can God be trusted? After the serpent insinuates this doubt about God's goodness into the minds of Adam and Eve, they yield to temptation. When Israel doubts that God's provision and guidance in the desert is really for their good, they yield to temptation. When we conclude that God is not good to us, that we have therefore to take matters into our own hands, then we have also succumbed to temptation.

"All good biography," claimed the twentieth-century literary critic Rebecca West in *Time and Tide*, "as all good fiction, comes down to the study of sin, of our inherent disposition to choose death when we ought to choose life." In the garden, the serpent lied to the woman when he told her that by eating from the tree she would surely not die. Banished from the garden, she and her husband Adam did die. The Israelites bitten by the fiery serpents in the desert were also dying. This brings us to our third and final point. We refer here to the sting of death. Only here there is a very remarkable turn of events: The people of Israel choose the second option. In response to the death-dealing serpents, Israel cries out: "We have sinned by speaking against God and against you. Pray to the Lord to take away the serpents from us" (Num. 21:7).

What happens next is mysterious. Moses makes a bronze serpent, places it on top of a pole, and lifts it up. Let us note its twofold significance here. First, it is a sign of God's judgment. Like the raising of a battle standard, this action presents to the people the one whom they are truly following: the serpent rather than God. It is a symbol of their rejection of God. The raised serpent is more than a sign of judgment. It is also a sign of God's victory over the serpent. Like the head of an enemy placed on the top of a pike and shown to the people, it shows that God is more powerful than the serpent. God is able to cure the effects of the serpent's poison. As a sign of God's victory, the bronze serpent shows God's compassion and desire to heal his people and do them good. We ought to take this to heart. Regardless of the trouble in which we find ourselves, God responds to our cries for help with grace, even when we've brought the trouble on ourselves, even when the mess we have made of our lives is our own. God's grace is not reserved for good people who need a boost now and again. God's grace is for those who have come to ruin by their own folly and rebellion. That is a remarkable thought, and it is at the heart of the good news.

Nowhere is this good news spelled out more explicitly than in our gospel lesson for today. Just as Moses lifted up the serpent in the desert, so also must the Son of Man, Jesus Christ, be lifted up. He too is both a sign of judgment and a sign of victory over death. When we see him lifted up on the cross, we are looking at the consequences of our mistrust and rebellion against God, consequences that he absorbed into his own body and thereby made his own. His cross is also the supreme expression of God's desire to heal and to do good to his people. God invites us, poisoned as we are by our sins, to look at him and live. "For God so loved the world that he gave his only Son, so that everyone who believes in him may not perish but may have eternal life" (John 3:16). Amen.

THE OBEDIENCE OF THE SON

HEBREWS 5:5-10; JOHN 12:20-33

Last time we dwelled on the ordeal of Israel in her sojourn in the desert. We saw that it tested the limits of her endurance. In her pain and frustration, she railed at God, seeing in him and his plan for her the source of her bitter misery. She believed the lie that God did not have her good at heart and rebelled against him. In short, she succumbed to temptation, of which the presence of the fiery serpents was the sign and evidence. In this regard, we stressed that the temptation repeated that of the original human pair. Adam and Eve were tempted by the serpent in the garden to doubt God's goodness. In succumbing to temptation, they broke faith with God and seized for themselves that which they determined to be good, instead of receiving it with an open and trusting hand from a good God. This proved disastrous for them, just as it did for Israel, and for every human being born into the world after them. In this we see that the ancient Hebrews were less concerned with the putative origins of the human race than with the condition of the human heart. We need not search for Adam and Eve in the mists of primeval history because they exist here and now in our own hearts. To quote Pogo: "We have met the enemy, and he is us."

Lest we be consumed by despair over our condition, let us recall that God showed Israel compassion. What is noteworthy in anticipation of the lessons appointed for us today is the role that Moses played. The people asked Moses to pray to God for them, that they might be healed from the poison of the serpents. Moses stood in the role of intercessor. This is an important term for us to bear in mind. It denotes one who stands before God on behalf of the people to plead their case with God. In the biblical world it is the priest who acts in the role of intercessor.

In our epistle lesson, the author wants to impress on us that Jesus is a priest *non pareil*. Moses acted in the role of priest for Israel in the desert, as we have already seen, but his significance for us consists in the fact that he points to our priest for all times and places. Our task then is to understand the claim that the author is making for Jesus our high priest. We can accomplish our task by playing the role of an interviewer. As an interviewer, we will ask about the credentials that qualify Jesus for this office of priest. First, we will ask about his heredity; then, we will proceed to ask about his character.

At first glance, it may seem odd to us that heredity should count as a requirement to be a priest. After all, we live in the age of democracy, in which the hereditary rights of kings no longer make sense to us. The basic point the author is making is that one cannot arrogate to himself this status. It is not a right that one can claim for oneself. Rather, it is an honor bestowed by another. In ancient Israel, one was eligible to be priest only in virtue of his membership in the tribe of Levi, which God had elected to serve him as priests. Now this poses a problem for the author of Hebrews. He is writing to Jewish Christians, who know that Jesus belongs to the tribe of Judah, and about that tribe God has said nothing about priests. The author then has to show that there is a greater, more authoritative priesthood than that of Levi. It lies in the cryptic figure of Melchizedek, whose name occurs in our lesson. We first meet Melchizedek in Genesis 14. When Abraham returns from the war of the kings, he encounters Melchizedek, who is called priest of God most high. His name means "king of righteousness," and he is identified as "king of peace." Melchizedek receives from Abraham a tenth of the finest plunder from war and gives him a blessing. What is happening in this scene? Melchizedek is performing the role of priest. But if only the descendants from the tribe of Levi were authorized to perform this role, to take tithes from their fellow Hebrews, how are we to understand Abraham's action? Later the author of Hebrews reasons that Levi himself, who receives the tithes, actually *paid* the tithes through the person of Abraham, because he was still in the body of his ancestor when Melchizedek came to meet him (Heb. 7:9, 10).

The conclusion is clear. Just as Melchizedek is greater than Levi, so also is his priesthood superior to that of Levi. God has appointed Jesus a priest forever, after the order of Melchizedek. In making this claim, the author has settled the question about Jesus' hereditary claim to the priesthood. This is not without irony, because Jesus is not a priest in virtue of physical descent, but in virtue of the power of an indestructible life (Heb. 7:16). He is always able to save those who come to God through him because he lives forever to intercede for them (Heb. 7:25).

Whatever we make of the argument that the author is advancing here, it may seem abstract to us. It is on the level of ideas. Granted, the Letter to the Hebrews is challenging, not least because it forces us to wrestle with difficult theological ideas. This should not obscure from view that our lesson concerns the life of a real human being, fully human even as fully Son of God, fully obedient to God even as he is in total solidarity with disobedient sinners.

This observation leads us to ask about Jesus' character. Let us first state the obvious. No doubt we can and should expect from one who performs the role of a priest integrity, inner strength, and moral probity. After all, the priest is to stand in God's holy presence. For this reason, the priest must be above reproach, of impeccable character. If not, he would be a scandal to the people and subject to God's judgment. Jesus possesses all this and more. No one could find him guilty of sin.

The priest cannot be entirely unfamiliar with the human condition, with the "heartache and the thousand natural shocks that flesh is heir to," to cite the memorable line from Shakespeare. What do we mean here? While we can admire strong people of firm resolve who always seem to achieve their goals, we may doubt they can ever understand us with all our struggles and failures and disappointments. "What does he know about it? He has never been through it." Or "How can she possibly understand? She has never known hardship a day in her life." This is not the kind of person we prefer to bring our needs before God. How can they even really know those needs if they can't relate to them? A young seminary graduate once told me about his experience interviewing at a church. "How did it go," I asked. "They liked me, but they told me to come back in twenty years after I had more life under my belt." That response doesn't seem entirely fair, especially if this young man had outstanding gifts for leading a church. And yet it is understandable enough. It expresses the thought that only when the young man's life has been tempered by his own suffering will he be in a place where he can relate to suffering people and thereby serve them effectively.

"In the days of his flesh, Jesus offered up prayers and supplications with loud cries and tears to the one who was able to save him from death, and he was heard because of his godly fear" (Heb. 5:7). Commentators tell us that this verse refers to the scene in the garden of Gethsemane when Jesus prayed to his Father to spare him from his impending death on the cross. Verse 27 in our gospel lesson also seems to allude to this scene: "My soul is troubled and what shall I say, Father, save me from this hour?" This scene does not exhaust these references. Jesus did not just experience anguish in Gethsemane but at other times during his life too. In the Gospel of Luke, Jesus already foretells the stress he must undergo: "I have a baptism to be baptized with, and how great is my distress until it is accomplished" (12:50).

John's Gospel also tells us that before the tomb of his friend Lazarus, Jesus was deeply troubled (11:33). His anguish is at its most intense at that moment on the cross when he cries out: "My God, my God, why have you forsaken me?" (Matt. 27:46; Mark 15:34). As the Son of God, who lived in constant communion with his Father, could it be possible that Jesus experienced suffering? The answer is an unequivocal "yes." This does not take anything away from Jesus' greatness. In fact, this is what makes him closer to us. As Hebrews says elsewhere: "Jesus had to be made like his brothers and sisters, fully human in every way. . . Because he himself suffered when he was tested, he is able to help those who are being put to the test" (2:17-18). This is a message of hope. The person who experiences anguish and trouble is no longer alone. He or she has one who understands and can relate.

Our lesson tells us that all this is necessary to make Jesus perfect through obedience. This raises a troubling series of questions. Is God's validation of his Son conditional upon his obedience? In our minds, obedience implies abject submission. Is Jesus then forced to accept God's plan in servile obedience to a will more powerful than his own? Does God want to crush Jesus beneath his will?

It may help if we consider that the root of the word obedience means to "hear or to listen well." In the Bible, listening is a very important element in the journey of faith. Every morning devout Jewish people say the *shema*: "Hear, O Israel, the Lord your God is one" (Deut. 6:4).

Jesus also needed to listen in order to understand God's plan in his life. Listening requires openness of mind and heart. Jesus was not coerced into doing God's will. Progressively, Jesus understood what it meant to be a true Son of God, how to live out his life in faithfulness to God, and did so freely in his humanity. This is what God sought from Israel from the beginning. It is in this that Jesus succeeds where Israel failed, where we have failed, as we have noted before. Our text tells us that Jesus' success did not benefit himself. By his act of obedience, he undoes our acts of disobedience and becomes the source of eternal salvation for all who obey him. Let us then now both in this Lenten season and always listen to him, following him on the path that leads to the cross, where he is truly himself, the compassionate and loving Son of God. Amen.

6

FRAGILE POSSIBILITIES, ROBUST HOPES

MARK 11:1-11

Karl Barth, the great Swiss theologian of the twentieth century, was moved as a child when his mother sung the hymns of the faith of the church. He became convinced that the stories of Jesus recalled in the hymns were those that might take place any day in his city of Basel. In fact, he achieved such certainty about the presence of Jesus that he spent an entire Palm Sunday, as a boy, watching for the entry of Jesus into his own city.

We can admire the zeal of the young boy, or wonder how his parents reacted to this unusual behavior, or even fear for what appears to be the boy's tenuous grip on reality. But we should not deny that the Jesus' entry into Jerusalem stirred up very powerful emotions among those present that day. It was an event filled with possibility. Is this the one we have been expecting? Will he deliver us from these Romans and their corrupt client kings who occupy our land? Will he establish the kingdom that God promised to his forefather David? Is this the moment on which the wheel of history will turn? Everything appeared to hang in the balance. Either God's kingdom would come with this man, or the people's hopes would be disappointed.

Jesus gave every indication that he was coming to do what the people expected. It is important to see that this whole event that is remembered on Palm Sunday is deliberately staged. It should be seen as a celebration of the return of a king or a conquering ruler. These celebrations were familiar in the ancient world. They followed generally a fourfold pattern: (1) the ruler was escorted into the city by the citizens or his army; (2) the procession was accompanied by hymns and acclamations; (3) objects were displayed to symbolize the authority of the ruler; and (4) a ritual was performed, usually a sacrifice in the temple, whereby the ruler symbolically claimed his authority over the city.

Do we not see this fourfold pattern in our narrative? Jesus' mount is that of a king in Jerusalem. The disciples knew exactly why Jesus sent them into the village to bring to him the colt. Before him, Solomon rode on a donkey on his way to be crowned king. Here the people acclaim Jesus in loud voices as the one who establishes the kingdom promised to David. The spreading of the cloaks along the road was a symbolic gesture to hail the king. The people cry out their hymns and acclamations. They joyfully praise God in loud voices for all the miracles that they have seen. Praise is the spontaneous response of gratitude and wonder from those who have witnessed God's redemptive power at work. Jesus' entry into Jerusalem to assume his rightful throne as king over the people of God would be the climax of all that he said and did among them. Jesus' reign as king will finally bring heaven's peace on earth and glory to God.

That Jesus is found alone at the conclusion of our narrative foreshadows how the city itself will receive her king. Jesus indeed enters into Jerusalem, but it is only to weep over its fate, because it did not recognize the time of God's coming to it. Jesus indeed goes into the temple courts, but it is not a symbolic act to claim his authority over the city. He goes to cleanse the temple, and to enact judgment on those who have turned it from a house of prayer into a den of robbers. This action enraged the rulers and religious authorities. This was the event that brought Jesus into fatal collision with them. From this point, they plotted how they might kill him. Later Jesus' authority is challenged. One of his disciples hands him over to his enemies. Finally, the Jewish and Roman authorities try him, and the latter sentences him to be condemned. He is tortured on a Roman cross, on which he cries out in a loud voice before his death: "My God, my God, why have you forsaken me?" (Matt. 27:46; Mark 15:34).

Jesus' entry into Jerusalem was a moment filled with *fragile possibility*. Reflect for a moment on who his followers were. The cloaks they spread on that road were not expensive garments; they were tattered shawls and dusty, sweat-stained rags. If Jesus was king, he was the king of the oppressed and the downtrodden. He had shared their hardships, healed their handicaps and diseases, and accepted them when the society rejected them as outcasts. Above all, he gave them hope and revealed God's love for them. They had come to march with him into the holy city—a victory procession! At the end of the week, on their way home, they would say to one another: "And we had hoped that he was the one to redeem Israel" (Luke 24:21).

Their last hope was riding on that borrowed donkey. Think about what might have been! The stage was set: If only Jesus had seized the moment, if only the people of Jerusalem had received him as they should have. If only God had fulfilled the dreams of those who followed Jesus. But now, what did it mean to follow Jesus? Or we might rephrase this in the present tense: "What does it mean to follow Jesus now?"

Our lives are filled with moments of fragile possibilities. A marriage that held the promise of lifelong happiness to which both partners eagerly looked forward—only to disintegrate under the impact of harsh circumstances neither of them really knew how to handle. An interview for a position that seemed an ideal fit to us—only to receive a phone call to tell us that we did not get the job.

Our lives are filled with moments when all seems promising, but then it just doesn't work out the way it should have. It can be so hard when life doesn't give to us what we expect. We don't know what God has in store for us. We don't know how he is leading us. To paraphrase Martin Luther, his involvement in our lives seems to be a strange work. If we become too impatient on the way, as did the people of Israel we encountered in the desert earlier in Lent, we are tempted to believe the lie that God doesn't have our good at heart. When people no longer perceive the hand of God in their lives, they speak of the absence of God.

But according to the Russian orthodox theologian Sergei Bulgakov, the absence of God should be translated as the silence of the Father. The people were right to raise their voices in praise of the one bringing the messianic kingdom. The God of Jesus Christ will not impose heaven's peace on earth by force. Roman medals in Jesus' day bore the inscription: "peace given to the world." This was the boast of Rome. The imperial court poet Virgil exhorted them in his famous epic: "But you, Roman, remember, rule with all your power the peoples of the earth—these will be your arts: to put your stamp on the works and ways of peace." But this was not the perspective of those that Rome conquered and plundered by force of arms. The historian Tacitus recorded the words of British chieftain Calgacus when he addressed a group of fellow soldiers: "The Romans create a desert, and call it peace."

This is not God's way. If Jesus is a king, he is not a king as the world understands the term. He does not come as the conquering warrior-king, but quietly on an animal that was the very symbol of peace. He is a servant king, willing to serve his people even to the point of giving up his life for them. Only this king can cut off the bows of the warriors and command peace to the nations.

In my student days, we read theologians who said: "God is different. God is other. If God is not different or other than who we imagine him to be, then he cannot be God. He can only be the projection of our desires." The God of Jesus Christ proves to be, in the words of Reinhold Niebuhr, not the "comfortable and convenient God of human expectations and categorizations, but God the Lord of heaven and earth." The events that led up to the cross prove to us that no one can comprehend the ways of a God whose wisdom is beyond searching out.

Christians throughout the world will call to mind in the days between now and Easter that there is no kingdom without a cross. Let us try to speak of this in human terms. Whenever we have experienced a loss or a disappointment, a friend or a family member may have come alongside us to give us words of wisdom. And they may have told us that whatever God did not give us, it is only because he is in the process of creating space in us to give what will be infinitely more precious to us. Have you ever heard it said that God never takes away something unless he plans to give something more valuable in its place? The old rabbinic saying, "The cow desires to give suck far more than the little calf wants to suckle," can be translated into religious terminology: "God desires to give far more than a person asks of him."

Is this not in keeping with the mysterious lesson that Jesus draws from the withered fig tree about which we read immediately after our narrative? Leaving Bethany to return to Jerusalem with his disciples the next day, Jesus is hungry. Seeing a fig tree, he goes to see if it has any figs. Seeing nothing on it but leaves, he says to it: "May no one eat fruit from you again" (Mark 11:14). Is this not a symbolic act that expresses the divine judgment of Jerusalem? This interpretation seems natural enough. But this is not what Jesus says about it. "Look, the fig tree that you cursed has withered," Peter exclaims (11:21). "Have faith in God," Jesus answers. "Truly I tell you, if anyone says to this mountain, 'Go, throw yourself into the sea,' and does not doubt in his heart but believes that what he says will happen, it will be done for him. Therefore, I tell you, whatever you ask for in prayer, believe that you have received it, and it will be yours" (11:22-24).

Does God really carve out space in us so that we can receive what he really wants to give us? "Do not be afraid, little flock, for it is your Father's good pleasure to give you the kingdom," Jesus assures his disciples (Luke 12:32). But they did not know then what they would know later. There is no kingdom without the cross.

Paradoxically, this remains our hope. With the people on the road into Jerusalem, we have seen fragile possibilities go unrealized. But our hope is robust, because now it can be grounded on God alone, who has done, is doing, and will do what we can never even have imagined.

"If you want to become everything you are capable of becoming, then become what he is." During Lent, we interpreted Jesus' summons to take up our cross and follow him along these lines. That total self-surrender to God means here in this life to have fellowship with his Son, even when this Son has borne a cross and died on that cross. This is what this time in the church year is designed to impress on us. We come to know that Good Friday is the last valley or last vale of tears on the way to the fulfillment of the life that God has promised: The peace of heaven on this earth, which will be renewed and filled with the glory of God. Easter Sunday lies ahead! Amen.

TO DOUBT GOD'S GOODNESS

LUKE 4:1-13

"For forty days, Jesus was tempted by the devil." The gospel lesson designated for this first Sunday in Lent certainly begins on a sinister note. For many, the very word "devil" evokes a shudder of fear. In popular imagination the devil is depicted as a malignant creature with horns and hooves and a pitchfork. He is associated with death and destruction, fire and everlasting torment.

As spooky or even as entertaining as this image may be for some, it does not correspond exactly to that in the Bible. To form a truer image of the devil, we have first to grasp his function. "Form follows function" applies no less to demonology than to architecture, as we will see.

Let us then begin by making an observation. The overarching aim of the devil is to make people doubt God's goodness. That is made clear in the story of the temptation of Adam and Eve in the garden in Genesis 3. God withholds from them the fruit of the tree of the knowledge of good and evil. As long as there is an implicit and unbroken trust in the goodness of God, there's no problem. There's no reason to be suspicious of the intention that lies behind the prohibition. Their relationship with their creator then remains open and free. That means they are open and free to enjoy God, each other, and all that God has made. Then the serpent, later identified with the devil, enters the scene. He asks the woman: "Did God really say that you must not eat from any tree in the garden?" (1). She struggles to clarify that it's only from the tree in the middle of the garden that they must not eat. But the poison of doubt has already entered into her heart. In his fine devotional *Dying We Live*, Eugen Drewermann helpfully paraphrases the serpent's question: "Did God make the whole world full of enticing possibilities to serve us in our quest for happiness, only to keep them out of our reach by forbidding them to us?"

We know how this story ends, because it never ends. It's played out again and again, generation after generation, in the heart of each man and woman born into this world. Drewermann points out that in our hearts we harbor doubt about God's goodness. God created a whole world, and it's a beautiful one, except for the fact what's most desirable in it is sinful. That's what our hearts tell us. Then religion intervenes to help us to be true to God—against our will, as we clench our teeth, convinced that to be on God's side means to miss out on the happy possibilities of this world. For this reason, we break the shackles that religion imposes on us. We go out into the world in search of alternative sources of happiness. We spend our lives in this restless search. We tap every well we can find. We find momentary satisfaction. But since it does not last, we continue the search. Yet we never entirely succeed in filling the emptiness. We cope by numbing out. We resort to substances or social media or dedication to more or less worthy causes. In the end, we struggle to suppress the nagging doubt whether life's really worth living at all.

This is an experience that's all too familiar to us and to our children and grandchildren after us. It's into this experience that Jesus Christ enters. Since he is one of us, he is subject to the same temptation to doubt God's goodness as we are. He's human, flesh and blood, as we are. That's why we find the devil with him too. The devil knows intimately the insatiable hunger of the human heart. It's to hunger that he appeals in the first of the three temptations of Jesus in the desert. It will be our task then to consider not only this one, but also the two that follow it, each in its turn.

Luke tells us that Jesus has been fasting for forty days; at the end of this period he is hungry. What ought to stand out for us here is the contrast between the garden where the devil tempts the first Adam and the desert where he tempts Jesus, the second Adam. In the garden, the first Adam is surrounded by beauty and love and abundance. Everywhere is evidence of God's goodness. But in the desert, Jesus is surrounded by chaos and loneliness and scarcity. These contradict the goodness of God. The Lord is God, and he created the heavens and the earth and put everything in place. He made the world to be lived in, not to be a place of empty chaos, according to Isaiah (45:22). In those moments when our world seems to us to be an empty chaos—that's when we are at our weakest. We should not imagine it otherwise for Jesus. The temptation to turn stones into bread—to do for himself what God would not do for him in a world that seems to be god-forsaken—this temptation comes to him at a very weak moment.

In addiction recovery programs there is an acronym, HALT. You may have heard of it. HALT stands for hungry, angry, lonely, and tired. Each one of these four conditions, when not recognized and addressed, leaves an individual vulnerable to relapse.

Whether or not we've ever struggled with a serious addiction, we know this to be true from experience. We are most vulnerable to temptation at our weakest moments, when we are hungry, angry, lonely, and tired. It's obvious that at least three of these four conditions obtained for Jesus. Yet Jesus does not succumb to the temptation, but resists it. This should lead us to ask: "How is it that Jesus succeeds where we fail?" The answer is that at no moment does his trust in God's goodness falter. That is why even in adverse circumstances, he can confidently wait on God, in whose word he trusts. Despite evidence to the contrary, he does not for a moment believe that God means him harm, but rather only good.

We then turn to the second temptation. Here the devil brings him to a high mountain and shows him all the kingdoms of the world. The devil promises to give him authority over all these kingdoms on the condition that Jesus bow down to worship him. Note that the devil targets in him his most vital concern, his deepest desire. He goes straight to the heart. To be king—this is the very purpose for which he is sent into the world. Here it is served for him on a plate.

The temptation is familiar to us. Let's say we have a good and noble goal. Achieving the goal is the desire of our heart. We even have the power at our disposal to achieve it. It will be a real benefit—not only to us but also to others. But we cannot attain the goal unless we compromise.

Consider, for example, the executive pastor who has a vision for his church. There are assistant pastors whom he regards as obstacles to its realization. They stand in his way. To remove them on a pretext immediately solves the problem. To be sure, there is collateral damage in the form of ruined careers and financial hardship for them and their families. But that's the necessary price to pay. That's how the world works. To succeed in this world, one has to learn to play by the world's rules.

In essence, this is the meaning of the devil's insistence that Jesus worship him. There's success in this world in serving the devil, since the whole world is in thrall to the power of the evil one, as John tells us (1 John 5:19). Conversely, there may be failure and hardship in this world in serving God. The personal cost for this success is high. When it turns to ashes in its time, those who paid the cost will realize they've been swindled. Jesus does not fall for it. "Worship the Lord your God and serve him only" (Luke 4:8).

After these two temptations, the devil is now convinced: There's no way to shake this man's uncompromising loyalty to God. There's need to change tactics. Therefore, he brings Jesus to Jerusalem, places him on the pinnacle of the temple, and challenges him to throw himself down. What is happening here? How are we to understand this third and final temptation?

The story in Genesis we considered at the beginning tells us that the serpent was the most cunning of all creatures that the Lord God had made. The devil demonstrates the validity of this observation here. Note that in none of these temptations is the devil godless, dangerous, or even disrespectful. He appears to Jesus as a devout man who can even quote the Psalms of David. What he is really attempting to do is to use the two responses that Jesus gave to the first two temptations against him. It's as if he is saying: "You said that you live only by the word of God, that you serve and worship God alone. Now here's your chance to prove it." The temptation then consists in the invitation to commit an act that demonstrates his radical trust in God. By throwing himself down, Jesus can show that he really believes in the promise of God to protect the one who trusts in him by sending the angels to rescue him before he's shattered by the fall.

The devil again goes straight to the heart. He perceives that loyalty to God is Jesus' most vital concern. To tempt Jesus to doubt his loyalty to God is also to tempt him to doubt God's goodness. If he fails here, then it will become clear that he doesn't really believe that God is worthy of his loyalty.

This temptation is also familiar to us. We succumb to self-doubt. We listen to the inner voice that whispers to us that our commitment to God is a sham. It tells us that we are not good enough. Or it tells us that what we've done in the past and even continue to do in the present makes us unacceptable to God. But that is also to doubt God's goodness. It's to believe the lie that God's grace and forgiveness are insufficient for us. This lie has to be recognized as coming from the devil. And when the devil lies, he speaks his native language, for he is a liar and the father of lies (John 8:44).

Jesus does not have to do the devil's bidding to prove that his heart is loyal to his God. He is secure in his trust in God and rooted in his knowledge of God's ways. He knows what to do and when to do it, which is the essential mark of the supremely confident man or woman.

"Submit yourselves to God. Resist the devil and he will flee from you" (James 4:7). One wonders if James had this scene in mind when he wrote to the recipients of his letter. The devil departs from Jesus, but only for a time; he will return at a decisive moment. Luke doesn't specify this moment, but one cannot help but think of those events that await us farther down this Lenten path we have just begun to walk together. There is another garden—not of paradise, but of Gethsemane, where Jesus' determination to do the will of his Father will be tested as never before. Then there are all the events of the following day, which we call Good Friday.

Until we arrive there and beyond, let us be sure to keep our hearts and minds ready and waiting for what God wants to impress on them in the weeks to come. Amen.

IN THE FACE OF OPPOSITION

LUKE 13:31-35

Last time we were in the wilderness with Jesus. There we found the devil with him. We recalled that the overarching aim of the devil is to tempt people to doubt God's goodness. This necessarily includes Jesus, since in his humanity he is one with us. If the devil had succeeded in tempting Jesus to doubt God's goodness, then Jesus would have denied his loyalty to God. After all, one cannot be loyal to a god one finds to be bad and untrustworthy. In that case, Jesus would have had to renounce the mission for which God had sent him into the world.

But Jesus did not renounce his mission. He succeeded in his contest with the devil. Yet the opposition to his mission did not cease. It continued. In the gospel lesson designated for this Second Sunday in Lent we find that he encounters it again. Only in this instance, it has a human face in the person of King Herod. Since it's our purpose in this Lenten season to retrace the steps that Jesus took on his way to Jerusalem, where he in fact does fulfill this mission, we have to pause here on the path to see what God wants to show us.

Let us begin with Herod. Herod is a client king subject to the emperor at Rome. He is charged to keep the peace in Galilee, the place where Jesus was raised and where many of his apostles came from. This is the same Herod who imprisoned John the Baptist and later had him beheaded. When Jesus learned of what had happened to John, he withdrew from the region, having recognized the existential threat that Herod posed to him and to his disciples.

Jesus' apprehensions are confirmed when the Pharisees bring to him the news that indeed Herod wants to kill him too. What motivates them to warn Jesus to flee? Is it concern for his safety? This is hard to imagine, given that the Pharisees are the implacable enemies of Jesus. They want nothing more than to remove him from the picture. Jesus' reply, in which he refers to Herod as "that fox," implies his suspicion that Herod sent them on a reconnaissance mission to gather intelligence about his movements. The Pharisees then would return to Herod to give him a full report, so that Herod can plan his next move. In this regard, Herod is attempting to be as sly or as crafty as a fox.

Opposition from authorities can make us unsure of ourselves and our cause. To be sure, many Jews considered Herod to be a usurper and therefore an illegitimate ruler, but he is no less the king. He holds high public office and upholds and enforces the law. If he wants to kill Jesus, it's because he sees Jesus somehow as a lawbreaker.

In more recent times, when Martin Luther King, Jr. went down to Birmingham to participate in a non-violent demonstration to protest the city's segregation laws, he was regarded as a lawbreaker and jailed. In his famous "Letter from a Birmingham Jail," he defended his actions. Not only was what King and the Alabama Christian Movement for Human Rights doing lawful, it was actually good for all residents of the city. If the authorities did not allow non-violent demonstrations, King insisted, violence would erupt. These demonstrations served as a pressure relief valve for a people under oppression. But even fellow clergymen in the city, who were white, incidentally, opposed King and his cause.

Herod's opposition to Jesus is unjust and even perverse. Why should anyone want to kill Jesus for freeing people from evil spirits and healing them of their diseases? What law is there against doing good? In another scene, Jesus is accosted by the Jewish authorities, who begin to pick up stones to kill him. Jesus asks them ironically: "I have shown you many good works from the Father, for which of these are you stoning me?" (John 10:32). By good works, he means such things as healing people of their diseases. Again, the point is clear: Opposition to Jesus is perverse.

We have already observed that when we are in adverse circumstances, when we face obstacles that seem to be insurmountable, we are more prone to doubt ourselves and our cause. It's in these circumstances that we need discipline. It is discipline that enables us to make good on our resolve to carry out a plan, like going to church, for example. There are many Sundays when it's an inconvenience or even a problem to go to church to worship. By sheer discipline, faithful attendees overcome obstacles and show up for worship.

But discipline has limits. We remain vulnerable to doubt ourselves and our cause. In fact, adverse circumstances can shake us up so badly that we may even begin to doubt the God who led us to espouse the cause and dedicate ourselves to it. Then our resolve to do what we know we should do begins to weaken. Our motivation begins to flag. Our energy and drive diminish. We feel like giving up.

We must not imagine that Jesus is immune from feelings of discouragement, since, as one of us, he feels everything that we feel. Only in this case, Herod's opposition serves to strengthen him in his resolve. This is indicated in an expression that at first seems puzzling. In his reply, Jesus divides up his plans in a three-day sequence. "Listen, I am casting out demons and performing cures today and tomorrow, and on the third day I finish my course" (Luke 13:32). He immediately refers to it again, even more cryptically: "Yet today, tomorrow, and the next day I must be on my way, because it is impossible for a prophet to be killed outside of Jerusalem" (33).

He cannot mean this literally, because there are many days yet until he arrives at Jerusalem. What then is he saying? Bible scholars tell us that the expression reflects a Jewish way of referring to a period of time that is filled with importance. That which is to be done in this period of time is so important that it has to be done in the order in which it is meant to be done. It cannot be otherwise, despite the forces that conspire to oppose and resist it.

Note that on the third day he's going to finish his course. The word in the original means to "reach a goal," with an emphasis on "completion" or "perfection." The same word appears in the account of Jesus' crucifixion in the Gospel of John. Before he dies, Jesus cries out from the cross: "It is finished" (John 19:30). Which is to say: "It is completed; it is perfected." This is the moment when Jesus can say that the mission for which his Father sent him into the world has been fulfilled.

But that moment has not yet arrived. There is still the pronouncement of judgment on Jerusalem. No less than in Herod and the Pharisees do we find opposition there too. Jerusalem kills the prophets and stones those that God sends to it. The holy city does not recognize the time of its visitation. It does not see itself as the destination point of the mission on which the Father sent Jesus. Therefore, it can only bring down on itself terrible judgment.

We cannot miss the thread that runs through this whole lesson. Everywhere we turn, we see evidence of the perversity of the human heart. It's in Herod, the Pharisees, and in all Jerusalem. We use the word "perversity" because it characterizes a heart that not only refuses to shun evil, but actively resists good. The perverse heart sees only evil in what is good, and only good in what is evil.

It's a pretty depressing picture. But the good news is that the gospel does not call us to battle with it. We can't anyway. In the gospel, it's clear that the people for whom Jesus came are armed and ready to do battle—not with their hearts, but with God. In Jesus Christ, God does not step into the neutral zone. He is in the middle of enemy territory. In our epistle lesson, the Apostle Paul tells us that many live as enemies of the cross of Christ. That is no less true today. But God does battle too. In opposition to the perversity of the human heart, God sets his own goodness and grace, for which our resistance is no match. The Apostle Paul grasped this. In his Letter to the Romans he writes that when we were still powerless, that is, when we were not able to help ourselves, Christ died for the ungodly. God demonstrates his own goodness to us in this: While we were yet sinners, Christ died for us; when we were God's enemies, we were reconciled to him through the death of his Son (Rom. 5:6-10).

Jesus anticipates this death. He knows that it is impossible for a prophet to be killed outside Jerusalem, as we have already heard him say. He must accomplish it there on the third day, as we have also seen. That is why Luke says elsewhere that when the day for this moment drew near, Jesus set his face like flint to go to Jerusalem.

Later in this Lenten season, we will be there with him. At first we will hear the people cry out with their hosannas on Palm Sunday to greet the humble king, who is the rightful heir to the throne of his father David and the legitimate ruler of his people—not Herod. Later we will hear from these same people the shouts: "Crucify him, crucify him!" (Luke 23:21). In this world, the hens and her chicks have not tended to fare well in their encounters with foxes. And even the chicks who stayed closest to Jesus will scamper away and scatter. But the hosanna will not be forever silenced. It will again resound. In many stern passages of scripture, into the darkest depths there shines a ray of hope. So also here. Jesus promises to return. At that time, his people will receive him with the acclamation: "Blessed is he who comes in the name of the Lord!" (Matt. 23:39). This is the last word in our lesson. It is on this word that we have to set our sight. For the reception of the king means life for the world and for all creation. In the meanwhile, let us find in him a sheltering wing under which we can gather together. Amen.

9

THE SEVERITY AND KINDNESS OF GOD

LUKE 13:1-9

The gospel lesson designated for this Lord's Day reflects an idea in the ancient world that persists to this day. We refer here to "karma." This is a word that should be familiar to most. Karma denotes the idea that the good things that we do in life will somehow boomerang back on us. We can expect good things. Conversely, the bad things that we do in life will also come back to us—but this time to bring us woe.

Bad karma—does this explain why the Galilean worshippers lost their lives at the hands of Pilate? Is this why the Tower of Siloam fell and crushed eighteen people to death?

Jesus does not endorse this idea. Those people were no worse than anyone else who has the misfortune to suffer a violent death. His summons applies to all equally: "Repent, or you too will perish" (Luke 13:3). Does this mean that Jesus is insensitive to us when we ask in our perplexity, "Why is this raft of misfortunes in my life? What did I do to deserve this?" No, but he also does not want us to be distracted by questions that we cannot answer. On the other hand, Jesus' very demand to repent implies that there is an order over which God rules: "Repent and you will live, refuse and you will perish." Of this Jesus is sure.

In Luke's Gospel especially, Jesus is portrayed as a powerful prophet. Jesus stands here in a long tradition of prophets in Israel. Consider the prophet Ezekiel's message to the exiles in his own day about 550 years before Christ. He tells them plainly that the soul that sins shall die. "Do I take any pleasure in the death of the wicked, declares the Sovereign Lord? Rather, am I not pleased when they turn from their ways and live?" (Ezek. 18:23). This finds an echo in Jesus' call to us to repent. If this call to repentance sounds severe or even harsh, it has to be read together with the parable that immediately follows it.

We have in this parable an image familiar to the world of the Bible. The vine was noted for its profusive foliage, intertwining branches, teeming shoots, and fragrant blossoms. But above all, it was the grape, whose harvest was accompanied by joy and celebration. The Psalmist extols the Lord for providing wine that gladdens the human heart (104:15). Similarly, the fig tree is a beautiful tree that produces a very sweet fruit more than once during the year. It provides shade and nourishment for the family it protects. It provides delicacies for the lovers in the Song of Songs, the love poem in the Old Testament. The vineyard and fig tree then together constitute metaphors for joy, peace, and prosperity.

In Isaiah, God compares his people to a vineyard (5:1-7). The image reflects God's will for his people. He intends that they be overflowing with joyful and abundant life characterized by peace and prosperity. But Isaiah complains that despite what God has done for them, the vineyard has not yielded fruit for him. For this reason, God threatens to remove its hedge, break down its walls, and let it be trampled down. For he looked for a crop of good grapes, but it yielded only bad fruit.

Nor is this a threat confined only to the Old Testament. In the New Testament, the author of the Letter to the Hebrews warns the faithful that the land that produces thorns and thistles is worthless and is in danger of being cursed. In the end it will be burned (Heb. 6:8). Later he reminds us that our God is a consuming fire (Heb. 12:29).

No doubt Jesus had the Isaiah text in mind when he related this parable. But note here that the owner of the vineyard does not carry out the destruction of the unfruitful fig tree that he threatened. His manager intervenes and pleads with him to leave it alone for another year. He promises to fertilize it in the hope that it will bear its fruit within a year. If after a year it still does not produce fruit, then the owner is justified in cutting it down.

The subject of this meditation is the "severity and kindness of God." Let us pause here and reflect first for a moment on what has been called the severity or sternness of God. Does this inform what we believe about the character of God? Do we appreciate that because God is holy and righteous and just, God must oppose the sin of those who stubbornly reject him, who willfully refuse to heed the call to repent? Do we realize that the imminence of God's judgment explains why this call is urgent? "Today if you hear his voice, do not harden your hearts" (Heb. 3:15; cf. Ps. 95:7). "Seek the Lord while he may be found, call on him while he is near; let the wicked forsake their way, and the unrighteous their thoughts. Let them return to the Lord, that he may have mercy on them … for he will abundantly pardon," Isaiah declares (55:6-7).

Then let us reflect for a moment on the kindness of God. Does this also inform what we believe about the character of God? Do we realize that it's the riches of his kindness, forbearance, and patience that leads us towards repentance (Rom. 2:4)? Do we realize that the kindness of God explains why this call to repentance can also be warm and winsome? "Listen, listen to me, and eat what is good, and you will delight in the richest of fare," as God speaks again through the prophet Isaiah (55:2). This accords with the words of the Psalmist, when he counsels, "Taste and see that the Lord is good" (34:8). Later the Psalmist follows his own counsel: "My soul is satisfied as with a rich feast, and my mouth praises you with joyful lips" (63:5). The Apostle Peter repeats this counsel in his first letter, when he urges us to crave the pure milk of the word of God, now that we have tasted and seen that the Lord is good (1 Peter 2:2-3).

In seminary, I remember learning the expression "time between the times." By this expression, my professors meant to say that we live between the first coming of Jesus Christ into the world, which we celebrate at Christmas, and the second coming of Jesus Christ, which we affirm in our recitation of the Apostles' Creed when we say, "from thence he shall come to judge the quick and the dead." This means that now, in the time between the times, we are living in a period of grace. The invitation to accept God's grace in Jesus Christ is extended to all now. In him God takes us, tends to us, and works in our lives through the Holy Spirit in order to make us a part of his healthy and fruitful vineyard. Our lives will overflow with abundant fruit as a result. And bear in mind that this remains God's will for us. "In the days to come Jacob will take root, Israel will bud and blossom and fill all the world with its fruit" (Isa. 27:6). That prophecy applies to us who are in Christ.

But to this invitation we need to respond as soon as it is extended to us. We cannot delay. If we have wandered from the truth and stand outside of the grace of God that is in Jesus Christ, we have to repent. Remember that the call to repent is how the Lenten season begins. On Ash Wednesday, the prophet Joel pleaded with us: "Return to the Lord your God, for he is gracious and compassionate, slow to anger and abounding in love, and he relents from sending calamity" (Joel 2:13). If we have heard God's voice in our lesson today, let us turn to him. We don't know how long the invitation will stand. We don't know how long the "time between the times" will be. Indeed, the longer we delay, the harder our hearts will become. We then risk losing the capacity to hear altogether.

But if we have already tasted that the Lord is good, if we are growing in his grace, if we are bearing fruit as a result of our union with Christ, then we ought to consider those who do not know him. As we have already mentioned, our lesson makes it quite clear that there's an urgency here. Do we have a friend or relative who needs to repent and turn to God? Perhaps at one time they attended church, showed an interest in the gospel entrusted to the church, expressed a longing to connect with God, but do so no longer. Have we prayed for him or her? More specifically, have we prayed that God, by the power of the Holy Spirit, would make them receptive to God's word, so that they may turn away from their sins and embrace the gospel, in which new life in Jesus Christ is found? Or have we sought the leading of the Holy Spirit within us for opportunities to talk to them about our faith? How about the people we know who are unchurched? We know that this is the fastest growing segment of the American population. They too need to hear the call to repent; they too need to discover for themselves the grace of God that is in his Son Jesus Christ. Many of them are seeking a new lease on life.

This gospel is a message of life and freedom. But our lesson has taught us that it is not only a word of liberation. To those who refuse it, it is a word of judgment. If people choose to reject it, they reject the kindness of God. The only thing left is the expectation of the severity of God's judgment.

Let us see that all have accepted the kindness of God as it is found in Jesus Christ. Let us pray for God's blessing in our lives, so that we may become fruitful fig trees in the Lord's vineyard. Then what we do and say will attract those to the God we worship. Then our witness to God's kindness will be effective. Then others will experience this new and abundant life in Jesus Christ. Amen.

RUNNING

LUKE 15:1-3, 11B-32

The gospel lesson designated for this Lord's Day features the parable of the prodigal son. No parable has generated more commentary than this one. Few scripture passages have inspired religious art more sublime than this parable has. Rembrandt's *Return of the Prodigal Son* is still recognized throughout the world, even in a generation not necessarily distinguished for its patronage of the fine arts. Called the "pearl of the parables," it contains a wealth of content to which we could easily devote four or five meditations. But we have only here to consider it. And so we have to choose a good point of access into the parable to ensure a broad view of the spiritual truths that it opens up for us.

Let us use for this purpose the image of "running." In the parable, Jesus tells us explicitly that the father runs to his returning son upon seeing him at a distance from his estate. That is remarkable in itself, as we will demonstrate in due course. Already someone may raise the objection: "We hear nothing about running with respect to the two sons, not to mention the rest of the characters in the parable." That seems to be a valid point, but hopefully it will become clear in the course of our meditation why the image of "running" seems to us to be the most appropriate one as our starting point. Let us then turn to the younger of the two sons. Before we do, let's speak frankly about what a modern-day prodigal might look like.

If we ask a modern-day prodigal about his past, it is always interesting to note the words he uses in telling his story. At one point, he may tell us that he began to run. At first, he ran to hide. This is no new phenomenon. Remember the source? In Genesis, we read that the Lord God came in the cool of the day to be with Adam and Eve. He called out to a hiding Adam: "Where are you?" Adam replied: "I heard the sound of you in the garden, and I was afraid, because I was naked; and I hid myself" (Gen. 3:9, 10).

We become afraid when something we did, or something done to us, makes us feel naked. Seeing no other option, we hide ourselves. That's how shame works. It drives us to hide. It convinces us that we are unpresentable to others as we are. That is why we understand when the modern-day prodigal tells us that he ran to hide from what he saw in himself. But at the same time, we understand that he does not run in place; he runs to something. He then tells us that he ran in restless pursuit of the next substance or sexual relationship or project or self-help program that promised to fill the emptiness. We understand that his running was fueled by an inner turmoil, a lack of peace and contentment. His inner life is a storm-tossed sea.

In the end, the modern-day prodigal was running from the self that he had become. To stop and turn around to face himself—that is just too painful. This explains in part why people resort to heavier doses of substances, or increasingly reckless behavior. They want to obliterate consciousness. They want to erase the self they have created. In more lucid moments, which become fewer and fewer as time passes, they want to "own their stuff." But they cannot summon the will power. Indeed, there is no power there, because the will is paralyzed by its bondage. But even if they were to turn it around, the burning shame presents an even bigger obstacle. Running now seems to them more like spinning, as in "spinning out of control." We realize that this is a very dangerous place to be. But it is to this place that this kind of running inevitably leads.

The younger of the two sons wants his share of the inheritance. That this is an act of rebellion is revealed in the request itself. In the ancient Near East, it is a supreme insult for a son to ask his father for his share of the estate while his father is still living. It was the normal custom for the heirs to receive their share at the death of the father. In effect, then, the younger son is telling his father to drop dead. Outraged, the father should have refused and punished the son. But he does not force his son into staying. In his love for him he has to let him go. He has to let him search for what he believes is lacking. Love is only love when it is freely given and freely received. The father wants the love of the son. But freedom is its necessary condition. Therefore, he has to let him go.

We cannot say that the son is literally running. But is this not a flight from home? In this sense, we are right in saying that he is running away from home. Moreover, it is a running to something, a flight into the far country. There the son descends into his own chaos of reckless living and wastes his substance and himself in the process. This is apparent in his taking of the job of swineherd. To the Jew, the pig is an unclean animal. This suggests that this son of a Jewish nobleman has lost his sense of himself. He no longer knows who he is. He's all alone and lives among the pigs. We realize that this is a dangerous place to be. But it is to this place that his running has led.

Then there is a turning point. Of the prodigal son, Jesus tells us that he comes to himself. Does that mean that he comes to an end of himself? In the drug rehab where I worked when I was very young, the counselors used to tell us that there is no hope for addicts until they come to the end of themselves. Only then are they ready to accept help. But are they? Not always. Perhaps "he came to his senses" is better, as some translations render it. Then it suggests that he is concocting a plan whereby he can cope with his shame. He will present himself to his father as a hired hand. That way he can reconceive his break with his father in terms of money lost. If he works long and hard enough, he can repay his father all the money that he wasted in the far country. Moreover, if he works as a hired servant, he will not be consuming his brother's share, since now the whole estate rightfully belongs to the elder sibling. Here is a plan whereby he can save both what is left of his pride and his life, threatened as it is by starvation. With new resolve, he rehearses to himself each sentence of the confession he plans to make to his father. At last, he heads for home. We now turn to the father.

We have already mentioned that the father runs. But, according to Kenneth Bailey in *Poet and Peasant*, a Jewish nobleman in flowing robes never runs anywhere. Aristotle tells us: "Great men never run in public." It is very undignified for them; it is a denial of their high stature. What then possesses the father to run out to greet the returning prodigal? Bailey explains that he wanted to protect his son from the abuse of the villagers, who would have come out to taunt him as he walked up to his father's estate. That is, the father was willing to humiliate himself to spare his son from further humiliation. But this is what love does. It covers shame.

Enveloped now in his father's warm embrace, the son begins to make the confession that he has already been rehearsing. The words in verse 21 and those in verse 19 are identical with one striking exception. "Make me one of your hired hands" is missing. In the embrace itself is a clear message: the father's refusal to accept him as he presented himself—a desperate and half-starved beggar willing to hire himself out for money. Everything the father does now for the son is meant to confirm him in his identity as his son. The best robe is no doubt the father's own robe, which he wore for feasts and special occasions. What better gesture can there be to convey the message: "You belong to me!"

The signet ring is a sign of trust. That the servants put shoes on his feet sends the clear message that they accept him as their master, not as one of them.

Love frees us from bondage. In the presence of total acceptance, we are free to be ourselves. To be sure, we will stumble, but love will pick us up and free us again and again. But what maintains us in our freedom is our new identity. The heart of the prodigal son has now become secure. He knows who he is in his father's love. He could return to live among the pigs. That is always a possibility. But the deeper he lives into his identity, the more uncomfortable that would feel to him. All this is the occasion for great joy. He lost himself but has been found. He was dead but is now alive.

The gospel could end here and all would be well, except at this point the scene shifts to the older brother. He cannot participate in the joy. He does not think it is fair. He stayed home and remained faithful to his father. He's the good son, but never rewarded for it. While his brother is treated to a feast of veal, he was never even given a goat for a small gathering with his friends.

The older son is right. He is good and upright. He is beyond reproach. He is the faithful churchgoer who never strayed. In him Jesus portrays the good and upright with due recognition and respect. But in him, we also see how this orientation toward life can lead to a worse place than the "born to be wild" orientation embodied in his younger brother.

In this connection, Eugen Drewermann asks: "Why is there so little freedom, joy, and understanding in the hearts of the good? Why do they see sin as a bit of happiness stolen from them?" The older brother fantasizes about how his brother must have spent his money. Nothing is mentioned about it before. But the older brother imagines it for us. He spent his money on "girls gone wild." This is very telling. He resents the fact that his brother realized the urge to freedom and adventure that he repressed. He seethes with envy and bitterness. To be good—that can be no more than the outcome of self-repression, of a life unlived. And it can disguise a cold heart, a joyless rigidity. The younger brother runs, the father runs, even the servants run at the command of the father to clothe the younger son in the dignity that he wants to restore to him. But the older brother is immovable. Drewermann is right in saying that no one can love God that way, no matter how good one is. No one who feels that way can call God "father" and mean it, not even one who sits in God's house for worship each Sunday.

It is troubling that the parable gives us no evidence that the elder brother ever changed his mind. We don't know if he ever joined in the celebration. In a certain sense, it is harder for the good to be saved than the sinners. That was and remains the offense of the gospel. At the same time, it is consoling that the father has the same love for his elder son as he does for the younger. He refuses to treat him as a hired hand, to reward him on the basis of services rendered. All that he has belongs to the son. How can it be otherwise in a relationship of love? Whether or not the older son comes to realize this does not change the father's heart. He is determined to celebrate and be glad.

Can we believe the words of this parable, which, according to Drewermann, are the most beautiful ever spoken in all human history? It is a message that still waits to be received and realized in this world. In Holy Week, we will discover that the elder brothers did not learn that one should return home where the music and dancing are; they decided rather that a man who speaks this way should be arrested, tried, and crucified because of such a reckless love. Drewermann insightfully points out that such a love reveals an inhumanity in the hearts of those who claim to be on intimate terms with God and yet know only the Lord God and never the Father, those who know the law by heart but never know mercy. Such a love reveals all our hearts. Let us not turn away from this revelation as we move deeper into the season of repentance through which Lent is leading us. Amen.

JUSTIFICATION BY FAITH

PHILIPPIANS 3:4B-14

Five hundred years ago, a young Augustinian monk named Martin Luther nailed 95 theses on the door of the Castle Church at Wittenberg, Germany, allegedly on October 31, 1517. His purpose was to present them for public debate among his fellow monks and professors. But in the age of the printing press they soon reached a broader public and seeded a largescale movement. For the most part, they concerned the sale of indulgences, by means of which the church offered to compensate for sins through payment of money. The indulgence authorized the purchaser to draw on the treasury of merits and good deeds accumulated by Christ and the saints and apply them to his own account, which was in arrears because of the bad deeds he had done. The indulgence restored the balance of his account. He then went on to live before God with a clear conscience, at least for a while—before incurring debt again.

Luther challenged this crass commercialization of Christian repentance. He later developed a theology according to which God's grace is unconditioned and free. God extends it to sinners and exacts nothing in return. People have only to hear the word of forgiveness announced in the gospel and receive it by faith. There is then no longer an account in arrears. There is no longer an account that has to be made whole by either the purchase of indulgences, or pilgrimages to holy sites, or fasting and penances. There is only freedom. Freed from the debt of sin, the Christian is freed for serving God and neighbor in joy and gratitude. This is what God wants for human beings. This is the deepest fulfillment of human beings, even if many no longer acknowledge it today.

For Luther this is the sum and substance of the gospel. For him it could not be otherwise, because if there were conditions attaching to it, conditions that we could not fulfill, then it would not be good news at all. Rather, it would be the sentence of our condemnation.

The epistle lesson designated for this Lord's Day affords us an occasion on which to revisit the insights into the gospel of Luther and the Reformers. More specifically, it provides us a window through which we can view and evaluate them with respect to their contemporary meaningfulness. To this end, I propose that we divide our meditation into two parts. In the first, we will attempt to answer the question: "How did Luther and the Reformers understand the gospel?" In the second, we will address the question whether this message is still relevant for us today.

We have been saying that according to Luther the gospel is received or appropriated or made one's own by faith. In this faith we stand before God as forgiven. Our sins are no longer charged to our account, in keeping with the metaphor drawn from the marketplace. This is how it appears from one angle. From another angle it appears otherwise. In this faith we also stand before God as justified. To be forgiven and justified constitutes one and the same reality viewed from two different angles. Let us pause to reflect for a moment on the word "justified." It may be helpful to recall that from Luther and the Reformers we have inherited an understanding of the gospel as justification by faith. What does this mean?

Let us begin by making an observation. God is holy, just, and righteous. But human beings are not. Luther was acutely sensitive to this problem, more than most in his age, so far as we know. How then do human beings become holy, just, and righteous? We may also pose this question in more familiar terms: "How do human beings become whole, perfect, and complete?"

The Apostle Paul expresses his desire for righteousness—but not for that of his own, which is from the law (Phil. 3:9). To Israel the perfection or completion of a human life is reflected in the law, which is summed up in the Ten Commandments. By conventional reckoning, the first four concern what we owe to God. We are to worship only him; we are not to worship idols. We are not to misuse his name. We are to honor him by keeping the Sabbath. The second six concern what we owe to one another. We are to honor our parents. We are not to murder, commit adultery, steal, bear false witness, or covet anyone or anything that belongs to another. These are the two tables of the law. The Ten Commandments constitute a blueprint for human life. If one were to live according to this blueprint, one would be a perfect, whole, and complete human being.

The problem is that no one keeps this law perfectly. Someone will object: "But one can always try harder. God will give an 'A' for effort." But if the standard is perfection, then this is not true and therefore is no consolation. And this realization was the source of Luther's anxiety and misery. After studying Paul's Epistles to the Galatians and to the Romans in the New Testament, Luther would come to the further realization that no one will be declared righteous in God's sight by the works of the law; rather, through the law we become conscious of sin (Rom. 3:20).

Now when we turn to our lesson in the Epistle to the Philippians, we see that Paul proposes an alternative to the works of the law. He himself was a Jew. Moreover, he was a Pharisee, one in a Jewish religious sect whose members were characterized by their uncompromising obedience to the law. Paul even distinguished himself among the

Pharisees. We read in the Acts of the Apostles that Paul studied under Gamaliel, the premier teacher of the law in the first century (22:3). So Paul submitted himself unfailingly to the law, in which he was also expert. He sought in this law the means by which to become perfect, whole, and complete. In biblical terms, in obedience to the law he sought righteousness.

But now he tells the Philippians that whatever gains he made here he now considers loss in light of Christ. He is now willing to lose all things for the sake of gaining Christ. "I want to be found in Christ, not having a righteousness of my own that comes through the law, but that which is through faith in Christ—the righteousness that comes from God on the basis of faith" (Phil. 3:9).

Righteousness in the sight of God does not come to us through what we do; it comes to us through what we receive. And what we receive is God's own righteousness through faith in Christ. We can now return to our question: "What is justification by faith?" God declares and accounts us as holy, just, and righteous in Christ by faith—this is the doctrine of justification by faith for which Martin Luther is known.

Now one may immediately raise the question here: "What role then do the Ten Commandments play in the life of the Christian? Are we to disregard the Ten Commandments since we no longer have to depend on keeping them to win God's favor?" This is a subject deserving of its own meditation. The short answer is this: "We don't keep them to make God favor us; God already favors us in Christ; so, God's favor makes us want to keep them." In this connection, we may note that this righteousness that he discovered in Christ did not make Paul slack. On the contrary, it released an energy in him; it gave him a new lease on life, so that his former zeal for the law now became zeal for Christ.

People ask whether or not the Reformation is relevant today. For me this is a variation on the broader question whether the Christian faith itself is relevant today. Let me suggest that it is, in virtue of the following considerations.

There is in the human being an inborn and ineradicable need for affirmation and esteem. It would be foolish to deny that we live in a time when self-esteem and self-affirmation are no longer relevant. In fact, I am not sure if I can remember a time when it has been more relevant than today. Bullies in schools tear down and destroy the self-esteem of their victims, even driving some to suicide. Cutthroat competition in the marketplace, in which there are always winners and losers, makes especially the losers question their self-worth.

The solution proposed by today's experts is to affirm or esteem or accept or love oneself. This advice is not entirely misguided. But it lacks a deeper basis or foundation on which I can expect to do this successfully. The message that Luther and the Reformers proclaimed so forcefully is that I can esteem and affirm and accept and love myself because of a prior act of God, in which God demonstrates that he esteems and affirms and accepts and loves me.

For Luther and the Reformers, this act is no less than Jesus Christ himself. What is bad and unacceptable in me God himself absorbs and thereby removes forever in the crucifixion of Jesus Christ. But God also shows that he unreservedly accepts and embraces me in raising this same Jesus from the dead. That God affirms and accepts and loves me—this is the basis on which I can affirm and accept and love myself. We may see this as a contemporary application of the message of justification by faith. And to the extent to which it is the case that we owe these insights into the gospel to Luther and the Reformers, it is legitimate to say that the Reformation remains relevant today.

Someone may object here that the Christian faith seems to be only for the weak. At first glance, that is a fair objection. After all, the bully sees no weakness in himself for which he has to compensate by working to build his self-esteem. And in history the church has provided a refuge for people otherwise denied a place in society. But I am not entirely sure that the two classes—the weak and strong—can be so neatly divided. In retrospect, I don't remember ever having met a successful man or woman who was entirely free from insecurity. In fact, in many—maybe even the majority—of cases, their drive for success was fueled by insecurity.

But the one justified by God through faith in Jesus Christ need never feel insecure. That person has been set upon an unshakable foundation. For this reason, that person can feel comfortable in his own skin. If God accepts him, then he can accept himself. No longer driven by insecurity, that person is freed to serve God and neighbor in joy and gratitude.

That message—that by faith in Jesus Christ God justifies us—released powerful impulses in the sixteenth-century church, even as it did in the life of the Apostle Paul, as he shared with those to whom he was writing at Philippi. May it also release powerful impulses in us here and now. Amen.

A ROYAL WELCOME

LUKE 19:28-40

The gospel lesson designated for this Lord's Day is read on a day significant in the church year. We refer here, of course, to Palm Sunday. On this day, Christians throughout the world make procession with palm branches in their places of worship. They do this to mark the occasion when Jesus rides into Jerusalem with a retinue of followers who proclaim him king. "Blessed is the king who comes in the name of the Lord!" as his disciples cried. The palm branch in Jewish tradition is a symbol of victory, at least since the time that Israel wrested political independence from the Seleucid empire at the hands of Simon Maccabee in 141 BC.

Throughout the whole season of Lent, we sensed the inevitability of this occasion. In Lent we learned again to be followers on the way. This is what it means to be his disciples. We also learned that this way leads to Jerusalem. In fact, the gospel makes it clear from the very outset that Jerusalem is the point of destination for Jesus. In the months immediately preceding his birth, we learned that in him God would raise a horn of salvation for his people in the house of his servant David. A few days after his birth, Magi from the East came to Jerusalem to ask about the one born king of the Jews, for they had seen his star in the night sky. In Jerusalem, the boy Jesus stayed behind, while his worried parents looked for him among family members and friends, not realizing that he had to be in his Father's house, by which is meant the temple in Jerusalem. In the face of death threats from that fox Herod, Jesus set himself resolutely towards Jerusalem, where his final confrontation with hostile authorities awaited him.

About the outcome of this confrontation we will learn later this week. Today we have only to acknowledge that he has arrived at Jerusalem. What does his entry into the holy city signify? For his people 2,000 years ago? For us today? Let us devote the space we have reserved for our brief meditation to the investigation of this twofold question.

For his people, the entry of Jesus into Jerusalem aroused an expectation. They were not ignorant of the meaning attached to the spectacle on display before them. Jesus' mount is that of a king in Jerusalem. The disciples knew exactly why Jesus sent them into the village to bring to him the colt. Before him, Solomon rode on a donkey on his way to be crowned king. The crowd of disciples acclaimed him in loud voices as the king who comes in the name of the Lord, as we have already seen. The spreading of the cloaks in front of him was reminiscent of how the people welcomed Jehu, after the prophet Elisha had anointed him king of Israel. Just as the people then cried out after Jehu, "Hail king of the Jews," so did the disciples cry out their hymns and acclamations. They joyfully praise God in loud voices for all the deeds of power that they had seen. Praise is the jubilant response of gratitude and wonder from those who have witnessed God's saving power at work. Jesus' entry into Jerusalem to assume his throne as king over the people of God would be the climax of all that he said and did among them. Jesus' reign as king would finally bring heaven's peace on earth and glory to God. Could this really be the promised Messiah, the rightful heir to the throne of David, the one who was to establish a perpetual reign of justice, peace, and prosperity?

We should not underestimate the urgency of this expectation. It became the more urgent the more the political circumstances worsened. Let me give you a mini-ancient history lesson, for which I am indebted to Marcus Borg and John Dominic Crossan, two New Testament scholars whose book *The Last Week of Jesus* details the final days of Jesus in Jerusalem. They remind us that the land of Judea was subject to Rome in Jesus' day. Now Rome placed the administration of their colonies in the hands of rulers chosen from local elites. In Judea these were the temple authorities. They came from wealthy families. In the ancient world, wealth came in the form of land ownership and the agricultural production it yielded. To accumulate wealth meant to acquire more land, usually through foreclosure and confiscation. That was common enough in Jesus' time. Subject to a triple tax structure—tribute to Rome, tax to the king, and a tithe to the temple,—many small landowners could not afford to maintain their holdings. Debt forced them to forfeit their land to the wealthy. Subsistence farming was then supplanted by large scale agricultural production for sale and export. Peasants who had once owned land became tenant farmers and sharecroppers, and the owners of large estates sought to work the land with as few of these as possible. Landless peasants had few options: day labor, emigration, or begging. Though by modern Western standards, peasant existence had always been precarious, it had been adequate. Now it no longer was.

The upshot is that Jerusalem's elites lived in luxury at the expense of the vast majority of the population, reduced to abject misery by exploitation. Conditions were intolerable. Understandably, there was a longing for a new order, for a new ruler—not an ordinary ruler, but one good and powerful enough to establish a reign of justice, peace, and prosperity. Again, was this Jesus the one to fulfill their expectation?

That was then and there, to be sure. But has the world really changed very much? Is the longing of these people in first century Judea so very different from our own? In a recent paper titled "Politics Beyond the Ego: Ethical Leadership for the Twenty-First Century,"

Duncan Enright decries a world where politicians rely on carrot and stick methods to impose their own agendas on peoples whose rights they are unwilling to consider; habitually exploit others to attain their own ends; and feel that rules are made for others and do not apply to them. Enright complains that these politicians are guided exclusively by self-interest. Re-election and the security of tenure, not the welfare of the people they represent, seem to be their priorities. Power and prestige, recognition and reward—these seem to be their primary concerns.

In contrast, according to Enright, the world needs political leaders who take account of the many different stakeholders; create a climate in which everyone can succeed and grow; and promote a culture of respect, equality, and hope for the future. Does not this expectation for such a leader border on a utopian fantasy? Or if not, how different is it from the expectation of a messiah? Our own situation may not be as desperate as that of a landless peasant in first century Judea. But in our political climate today, many are agitating for a new order, having withdrawn their trust from the one they see as destined to decay. Witness the angry riots and demonstrations in the streets of our cities and the hateful vitriol on social media.

The next question, naturally, is how does Jesus respond to this expectation? The manner in which Jesus enters Jerusalem should have given the disciples a clue. The meaning of the spectacle is clear, for it recalls a prophecy from Zechariah. According to Zechariah, a king would be coming to Jerusalem, "Humble and riding on a colt, the foal of a donkey" (9:9). In Luke, this reference to Zechariah is implicit. But it is instructive to refer to this Old Testament text. The rest of it details what kind of king he will be. "He will cut off the chariot from Israel and the war-horse from Jerusalem, and the battle bow shall be cut off, and he shall command peace to the nations" (9:10). This king, riding on a colt, will banish war from the land—no more chariots, war horses, or bows. Commanding peace to the nations, he will be the king of peace.

The opposition of the Pharisees to the spectacle foreshadows for us how the city itself will receive this king. "Rabbi, silence your disciples," the Pharisees demand. Jesus indeed goes into the city, but only to lament over its fate, because it did not recognize the time of God's coming to it. Jesus does goes into the temple courts, but it is not to wrest authority from a corrupt priesthood. He goes to cleanse it and to enact judgment on those who have turned it from a house of prayer into a den of robbers. This action enraged the rulers and religious authorities. This was the event that brought Jesus into fatal collision with them. From this point they plotted how they might kill him. Later Jesus' authority is challenged; one of his disciples betrays him to his enemies; and finally, the Jewish and Roman authorities try him and sentence him to be condemned to a violent death.

It was a violent world then; it is a violent world now. Rival claimants to political office do not hesitate to resort to violence to seize power. The old order has to be destroyed to be replaced by a new one. Throughout history nations have had their warrior gods. They invoke these gods to grant them victory over their enemies. They go out to fight in the name of these gods.

But we are right in asking the question whether these are really gods at all. How does this violence in which we are all engulfed really relate to God? In the strict sense, violence does not originate in God, but in our disordered relation to God. This in turn results in a lack of peace in the human heart. How to restore peace to the human heart—that seems to me to be the prior question, one that applies both to then and now. For it is the perennial question, to which all the religions and philosophies and self-help programs of the world have sought an answer.

The church fathers reflected on the symbolic significance of the colt. They asked how it was possible for anyone to mount an uncastrated young male horse on which no one has ever ridden before. They could only conclude that the one who sat on it on Palm Sunday has the power to bring untamed forces under his sovereign control. Among these forces we have to name above all is human violence. To see how God extinguishes violence among us we have to look at the cross. There Christ absorbed human violence in himself and thereby neutralized it. There he reconciled human beings to God and to one another, making peace through his shed blood. This is the good news of Good Friday, which awaits us later this Holy Week.

Can we remain faithful to this message, despite living in a world where violence continues? Returning again to the church fathers, we note with them the stubbornness of the colt. However long violence in this world continues, it cannot have the last word. Christ's mount is stubborn and will outlast it. He can and will because he is Lord of all. Our epistle lesson makes this clear for us: it tells us that as Jesus humbled himself by becoming obedient to death—even death on a cross, God exalted him and gave him the name that is above every name, so that at the name of Jesus every knee should bend, in heaven and on earth and under the earth, and every tongue should confess that Jesus Christ is Lord, to the glory of God the Father (Phil. 2:8-11). Amen.

13

NEED, TEMPTATION, OBEDIENCE

MATTHEW 4:1-11; ROMANS 5:12-19

Today our Lenten journey begins. Since the season of Lent consists in a forty-day period that we mark out from those special events in our redemption that culminate in Easter Sunday, our gospel lesson appropriately places us in the desert with Jesus, where he undergoes a forty-day fast. This, in fact, precedes his encounter with the tempter, also known as the devil or Satan.

The drama that unfolds is familiar to many of us. We find Jesus in need. We know that when we are in need, we are at our most vulnerable to temptation. The devil knows this too. That is why he sees this as an opportune time to tempt Jesus. He attempts to persuade Jesus to appeal to his relationship to his God and Father and his special prerogatives as the Son of God to satisfy his need. After all, Jesus is a powerful king who is to inherit a kingdom that is universal in extent. But to exercise his office he needs nourishment as well as the assurance that his God will protect him and establish his reign. Indeed, in this perspective the actions that the devil proposes are good and legitimate. They are in keeping with what is expected from the Son and therefore what the Son should expect from his God and Father.

But there is a catch. To satisfy his need, Jesus has to hear and obey a voice other than that of his Father. Of course, we refer here to the voice of the tempter. This he will not do. For this reason, after each of the temptations, he turns to the scriptures, in which he hears God's voice, a voice which he must hear and obey rather than that of the devil. He will trust his God to supply all his needs and fulfill his purposes for him.

Let us pause here momentarily and ask: "What does it mean to be tempted?" When we reflect on the phenomenon of temptation, we see that it is conceived in doubt. We have a legitimate and even pressing need. We bring our need before God in prayer. We wait expectantly, but God neither meets our need in us nor us in our need. He is silent.

Time passes, but our need does not. In fact, it becomes even more pressing. We pray more fervently, but there is still no answer. Our hearts become less confident. Before long, we doubt that God hears our prayers, that God even cares at all about our need. Then temptation intervenes and whispers to us that God does not provide for us, that therefore God must not love us.

We muster up what little defenses we have to resist this temptation, but it proves to be too overpowering. We succumb to it. If we are resourceful and know how to play by the world's rules well enough, we may satisfy on our own the need about which we prayed to God. But we are heartbroken. We are disappointed in God, because he abandoned us in our need, and we are disappointed in ourselves, because we proved too weak to resist the temptation. And in succumbing to the temptation, we incurred guilt, because instead of receiving what we needed as a gift from God's generous hand, we seized it on our own, apart from God's will.

Did Jesus ever doubt? Not only in the desert, but also at those hard moments in his life when it must have appeared to him that his God and Father was neglecting him and thereby abandoning him in his need?

In fact, the scriptures present to us two paradigmatic moments here. The first is in the garden of Gethsemane, where Jesus falls down on his face before the Father before his arrest, trial, and crucifixion. "My Father, if it be possible, let this cup pass from me. Nevertheless, not as I will, but as you will" (Matt. 26:39). In his version, Luke tells us that he was in such anguish that his sweat became like drops of blood, falling on to the ground (Luke 22:44). The second is the crucifixion itself. On the cross, Jesus expires with a cry of dereliction: "My God, my God why have you abandoned me?" (Matt. 27:46; Mark 15:34).

These passages are as comforting as they are difficult. At the very least, they show us that Jesus has known and experienced the anguish of our doubt and made it his own. But even more comforting is that his doubt did not bring him into that disastrous place where it does us: the breaking of our faith with God. In those agonizing moments when we doubt that God has our best at heart, that God is still good to us despite all appearances to the contrary, we can and often do break faith with God and believe the serpent's lie. In those moments we fall prey to temptation and sin. For anything that is not of faith is sin (Rom. 14:23).

In our epistle lesson appointed for today, the Apostle Paul paints this contrast between us and Jesus on a very broad theological canvas. There he divides all humanity into two distinct camps. Let us see if we are able to follow Paul's somewhat complex argument here.

Over the first camp stands Adam. Of course, we encounter Adam first in Genesis. He is the first human being, whom God created from the dust of the earth and placed in the garden of Eden to till and keep it. But there, together with his wife Eve, whom God had fashioned from his rib, Adam succumbed to temptation and disobeyed God. In the context of Paul's argument, Adam is not a lone figure. He is at the same time the human race. Or, more accurately, he stands as the head and representative of the human race. That is why, from Adam's disobedience, which each of us repeats and makes our own, come sin, condemnation, and death to us all. In this connection, the famous line from Benjamin Harris' 1690 New England Primer applies: "In Adam's fall, we sinned all."

Over the second camp stands Christ. As the last Adam (1 Cor. 15:45), he supersedes the first Adam as our new head and representative. Christ overcame temptation and obeyed God's word, as we have already seen. He did this alone and for himself. But as our head and representative, he also did it on our behalf. In virtue of what Christ has done on our behalf, instead of sin, condemnation, and death, we receive all that flows from his life of perfect obedience, through faith.

Paul stands amazed at the magnitude of Christ's saving power. He observes that his one life, lived in perfect obedience to God, undoes the consequences of so many lives—too many to count—that have been lived in disobedience to God. The trespass is not like the gift. For while "the judgment followed one sin and brought condemnation, the gift followed many trespasses and brought justification" (Rom. 5:16). This is a variation on a theme in Romans: where sin abounds, grace abounds all the more (Rom. 5:20).

Paul sums up the contrast between us and Christ in these words:

> *Consequently, just as one trespass resulted in condemnation for all people, so also one righteous act resulted in justification and life for all people. For just as through the disobedience of the one man the many were made sinners, so also through the obedience of the one man the many will be made righteous* **(Rom. 5:18-19).**

Jesus' perfect obedience is an aspect of his person we ought always to keep before us. He was unwavering in his commitment to live before God and with others as God's faithful covenant partner. He consistently upheld the demands of love and justice embodied in God's commandments, even in the anguish of temptation, even in the face of opposition from evil men, who unjustly condemned him (1 Peter 2:23). In his humanity, Jesus, the Son of God, steadfastly rendered the obedience to God that we owed, but failed to give. Jesus not only did this apart from us, but also for us and on our behalf. In the days leading up to Jesus' arrest, trial, and crucifixion, which we will observe during Holy Week, it will become even clearer to us that Jesus lived the life we were meant to live, but didn't, and died the death we should have died, but didn't. Then we will understand what theologians call the "wondrous exchange": Jesus gives to us what is his and takes on himself what is ours.

Today we renew our commitment to follow Jesus on the way. That way begins in the desert, the place of temptation. But let us not fear, because the one who goes before us has overcome temptation, defeated the devil, and rendered perfect obedience to God on our behalf. And if while in the desert we are burdened by our need and feel vulnerable to temptation, we can turn to him. The author of the Letter to the Hebrews tells us that Jesus was tempted in every respect as we are yet was without sin (4:15). The author invokes this precious truth to assure us that we don't have a high priest who is unable to sympathize with us in our weakness. He knows what it's like. That is why we should not hesitate to go to him to obtain mercy and find grace to help us in our time of need (4:16). Amen.

IS THERE HOPE EVEN FOR ME?

JOHN 3:1-17

Students of the lectionary have observed that the gospel lessons appointed for this season of Lent intend to present to us portraits of conversion. The subjects include Nicodemus, the Samaritan woman, the man born blind, and Lazarus, whom Jesus raised from the dead, as well as his sisters Martha and Mary. If indeed this is its intent, it does not appear at first glance that Nicodemus qualifies. There is no evidence to suggest that at the end of his extended conversation with Jesus, Nicodemus is any closer to believing that Jesus is the Son of God than he was before the encounter. On the contrary, this "teacher of Israel" fails to grasp even the most basic of spiritual truths. That failure stems from a heart that obstinately refuses to accept the testimony from God about his Son, because that heart is closed up in unbelief.

To be sure, we are not misguided in arriving at this verdict on Nicodemus. It is, after all, based on solid evidence to be found in our lesson, open for all to see. Nevertheless, if this verdict remains unsettling to us, if this case is difficult for us to lay to rest, there are good reasons, also to be found in our lesson. In fact, on closer analysis, Nicodemus appears to be a rather complex character who is less antagonistic to Jesus than this verdict supposes.

In support of this claim, let us consider the following. Nicodemus deferentially addresses Jesus by the formal title "Rabbi." He acknowledges that the signs that Jesus has performed authenticate him as a teacher who has come from God. Perhaps he comes to Jesus at night because it is the time when Jesus will be free from the distractions of the day and therefore able to give this seeker his undivided attention. If this is so, then Nicodemus can be seen as a man genuinely interested in learning more about Jesus and his teaching.

Further support for this claim can be found later in John's Gospel. When the Pharisees and the chief priests expressed frustration at the officers for failing to seize Jesus, Nicodemus spoke up on Jesus' behalf (7:50-52). When Joseph of Arimathea removed the body of Jesus from the cross to prepare it for burial, Nicodemus came to him with spices for the embalming, a mixture of aloes and myrrh totaling one hundred pounds (19:39-40). This represents an enormous expense, which we can hardly imagine to be borne willingly by someone who did not at least sympathize with Jesus and his mission.

But in our lesson Jesus does not appear to return this sympathy. He does not recognize himself in Nicodemus' characterization of him, and abruptly tells him so. Evidently, what Nicodemus has said to Jesus is not in conformity with the truth. Nor can it be unless it is preceded by a new birth. For no one can see the kingdom of God unless he is born from above. This is what Jesus tells him.

This evokes from him the response: "Can a man be born when he is old? How can a man enter a second time into his mother's womb and be born?" (John 3:4). Nicodemus' question is poignant. He's grown old. With age comes experience. No doubt the lessons he has learned from experience have been hard won. They have taught him how to accommodate himself to the world and the world to himself. Would not reverting to a period in which he has to enter this world for the first time mean forfeiting what he has learned from those lessons? How is that possible or even desirable? He has already so much invested in them. They make up who he has become. To let them go is to let go his sense of self, to which he must necessarily cling if he is going to maintain himself in his own eyes and above all in those of the world. Viewed from this perspective, Nicodemus' question does not betray the depth of his spiritual obtuseness; on the contrary, it reveals the depth of his awareness of human limitations.

What about us? Are we any different than Nicodemus? When we are young, our hearts are innocent. Soon we launch out on our life's path. We meet a variety of people. We travel to different places. We become exposed to new ways of thinking about the world. To be sure, this is normal. In fact, without it we don't evolve into mature adults; we don't realize our full potential. On the other hand, when our path leads us into cul-de-sacs, when we become exposed to too much that is harmful to us, when we accumulate too much baggage, then our hearts lose their innocence. And then, sooner than we anticipated, we too have grown old. We certainly gained experience, but along the way we lost our capacity to see the kingdom of God. No less to us than to Nicodemus, then, do the words of Jesus apply: "You must be born from above" (John 3:7).

Parenthetically, it is on the basis of these words Jesus addresses to Nicodemus that many well-meaning Christians have approached those with whom they want to share their faith with the question: "Are you born again?" The irony is that the appeal these Christians are making presumes that their interlocutors should "get" born again, if in fact they cannot answer that they already are. These Christians miss the pathos of the exchange in our lesson, for to be "born again" is, as Nicodemus rightly recognizes, humanly impossible.

At this point, Nicodemus stands exactly in the same place as the rich young man after his exchange with Jesus (Matt. 19:16-25; Mark

10:17-27; Luke 18:18-27). In search of wisdom, he too eagerly comes to Jesus, whom he recognizes as an authority. He wants to know how he can inherit eternal life. At first, Jesus gives an answer that one ought to expect from a Rabbi: "Follow the Ten Commandments." The man responds that he has kept them all from his youth. Then Jesus tells him to go and sell all his possessions and follow him. But this the young man could not accept. He goes away sad, finding it impossible to do what Jesus is requiring of him.

Jesus reflects on his encounter with the young man. "How hard it is for a rich man to enter into the kingdom of God. It is easier for a camel to go through the eye of a needle that for someone who is rich to enter the kingdom of God" (Matt. 19:24; Mark 10:25). The disciples pose the right question: "Who then can be saved?" Indeed. Is there any hope for the rich man? For Nicodemus? Is there any hope for us? Jesus replies on that occasion: "With you it is impossible. But with God all things are possible" (Matt. 19:26).

Returning to our lesson, we note that Jesus develops his statement, "You must be born from above," by introducing the Holy Spirit. In fact, in the Holy Spirit lies the interpretive key that opens up the meaning of the statement, "With God all things are possible." These things include even and especially new births, which are the same as new beginnings.

In the Spirit, God makes new, begins again. In the very beginning, God's Spirit hovers over the face of the deep. Here the deep stands for all kinds of threats that can devastate the earth. Combined with the darkness, it is a menacing presence. But it is there that the Spirit brings forth, giving the world a generous and good face.

Later God's Spirit is there at the chaos after the destruction of Jerusalem and the desolation of the Promised Land. In the prophet Ezekiel's vision, the house of Israel lies scattered like bones over the desolate expanse of the desert floor. "Our bones are dried up; our hope has gone; we are cut off completely," the people complain (37:11). With them it is impossible. But it is there that God's Spirit recreates, knitting bones together, forming flesh, and breathing new life into corpses, giving the promise of a new beginning on their own soil.

In a new beginning, God's Spirit hovers over the Virgin Mary. And in the one to whom she gives birth there is the promise of a new creation. In the Gospel accounts, however, Jesus meets a violent end at the hands of his enemies. He is buried in a tomb. But there too God acts to give new life. It is by the power of the Spirit that God raises this Jesus from the dead.

And then the nations, which had been dispersed over the face of the earth after attempting to form one people at Babel, are brought together again at Jerusalem— this time finding a firmer basis for their unity in the one crucified and risen. Once again, it is the Spirit that makes this possible, having been poured out on Jesus' followers at a Pentecost festival there in fulfilment of the prophet Joel's prophecy: "I will pour out my Spirit on all flesh" (2:28; Acts 2:17).

This event anticipates eschatological fulfilment on that great day of the Lord's coming, accompanied, according to the Apocalypse of John, by the announcement of the one who sits on the throne, "behold, I am making all things new" (21:5).

These new beginnings in the Spirit are found throughout the scriptures, as we have tried to sketch here. They together form a pattern of God's mysterious action in the history of God's people, whenever and wherever God wills. For the wind blows where it wills, and though we hear the sound, we cannot see where it comes from or where it is going (John 3:8). So it is with the Holy Spirit.

When the possibilities for the future are obscured by a hopeless present, when the options of men and women are exhausted, when projects fail and plans meet with frustration, God's Spirit is there. He is creating new beginnings.

Let us then watch and wait expectantly for these new beginnings, hopeful in the God who acts mysteriously in our lives, in our churches, and in our world through the Spirit. Amen.

SEARCH FOR SATISFACTION
JOHN 4:5-42

Jesus is the *incarnate* Son of God, meaning that in every way except sin he is a human being like us. That is why he can experience fatigue and thirst, as he does on his return to Galilee from Judea through Samaria. The heat from the midday sun bears down on him, sapping him of his energy, and prompting him to sit down to rest by a well. Soon there appears a Samaritan woman, whom he decides to ask for a drink.

This would be a non-event for us today, escaping our notice. But Jesus is a Jewish man, his counterpart is a Samaritan woman, and this is the first century. There exist three layers of division between them.

The first is political. The breach opened up between Jews and Samaritans at the time of the exile of the Northern tribes of Israel with the Assyrian invasion. The Jews who remained in the region of Samaria during the Assyrian occupation adopted the customs of their captors and intermarried with them.

The second is religious. Because they became impure by intermingling with the Assyrians, they were forbidden from entering the temple in Jerusalem; so they built their own on Mount Gerizim. Later, when the Samaritans withheld their support from the Jewish people in their war of independence, the Jews retaliated by destroying their temple. Subsequently, the Samaritans returned the favor by attacking the temple in Jerusalem, defiling it by scattering the bones of the dead in the sanctuary. To make matters worse, in Jesus' day, Samaritans were known to waylay Jewish pilgrims traveling to and from Jerusalem. To be called a "Samaritan" was a supreme insult to the Jew. Samaritans were defiled and Jews risked defilement in handling anything belonging to a Samaritan. Thus, the one chosen people stood divided in Jesus' day. No self-respecting Jew associated with a Samaritan.

But there was one last layer of division between Jesus and the Samaritan woman. As a man in orthodox Jewish society, it would have been improper to ask a Samaritan woman for help, let alone engage her in conversation. What Jews believed about a man and a woman conversing in public is embodied in the Rabbinic wisdom prevalent in Jesus' day, as expressed in this saying: "A man shall not talk with a woman in the street, not even with his own wife, on account of what others may say. He that talks much with womankind brings evil upon himself. If any man gives a woman a knowledge of God's Law, it is as though he had taught her lechery." That perhaps explains why, when they returned, the disciples were astonished to find him talking with a woman. Nothing of the dialogue would have taken place if Jesus had not the courage to cross the boundaries created by state, religion, and gender.

Jesus asks the woman for a drink. We know that in John's Gospel Jesus uses material realities to communicate spiritual truths. It's no different here. Water is a material reality. It is something we can see, hear, touch, taste, and smell. It is the source of life. It sustains us and renews our strength. But that is exactly why it is such an apt vehicle to communicate the deeper spiritual truth that Jesus himself is. If we don't see how Jesus uses the woman's desire for water to open up a deeper conversation about desire and where the satisfaction of our deepest desire can be found, then we miss the point of the whole narrative.

Let us then begin by stating the obvious. To thirst is to desire. Jesus desires a drink. The woman comes to the well because she is drawn by her own desire. That is to say, she has to satisfy her own thirst, as well as that of her family members and animals. The desire for water is most basic. In fact, when we are parched, our desire for water takes precedence over all the others. The satisfaction of *this* desire is first in order of importance.

Water then refers us to human desire, to our desire. Indeed, desire is a subtext that runs throughout this lesson. We learn that the woman with whom Jesus interacts at the well is a woman marked by desire. She desires the water that Jesus promises to give her, the water that satisfies so completely that the one who drinks of it will never be thirsty again. But when Jesus sends her to fetch her husband and come back, there emerges a more complete picture of who she is as a woman marked by desire.

"I have no husband," she replies. "You are right in saying you have no husband. In fact, you have had five husbands, and the one you have now is not your husband" (John 4:17, 18). Sexual intimacy holds out to us the promise of satisfying our deepest desire. This is a truism that applies at all times and in all places. It especially applies in our own, where sexual promiscuity in the "hook-up" culture is rampant. In this regard, the Samaritan woman is strangely contemporary with us. But Jesus does not bring up her past to judge her. God did not send him into the world to condemn her and those of us like her, but to save her and those of us like her through him. The point is to show that it wasn't sex or meeting her soulmate or finding companionship, as good and as desirable as those things can be, that would ever satisfy her deepest desire.

The woman does not withdraw from Jesus in shame, as one might expect, but engages him in spirited conversation. She knows the religious traditions of her people. She is conversant enough in theology to pose intelligent questions. Is it not often the case that the most passionate people we meet are also at the same time the most ardent spiritual seekers? Does not this seem to be a contradiction? The wisest students of human nature teach us that there is a sensitive interface between our sexuality and our spirituality. The strands of erotic desire and spiritual aspiration are not always so easy to separate in the human heart. This perhaps makes sense of the old saying that when a man knocks at the door of a brothel, he is really looking for God.

The dialogue comes to a conclusion. We all want to know the moment when the woman comes to the realization that in this one, this Jesus, she has found the satisfaction of her deepest desire. That this encounter transformed her is clear. How else can we explain the zeal with which she goes from door to door throughout her town to tell everyone about the man she met?

The clue lies in what she says to the people in the town: "Come and see a man who told me everything I have ever done" (John 4:29). Why is this significant for her?

A marriage therapist shared her discovery in her practice that a major cause of marital strain is the failure of spouses to listen to each other. When our loved one chooses not to listen to us, we feel misunderstood. If this becomes chronic, we begin to feel that the one closest to us does not really know us—or worse yet, even care to know us. This is why people can feel profound loneliness within this closest, most intimate of all human relationships.

Not too long ago, we began to hear in the media about the "loneliness epidemic." This expression became commonplace when the government of the United Kingdom a couple of years ago declared loneliness a public health crisis and appointed at that time a minister of loneliness to coordinate a response to it. It is well-known that loneliness can give rise to disturbed behavior, including self-harm. When asked why she cut herself, one young woman replied that the lonely have no one to give witness to their existence and therefore live with the fear that there will be no record of who they were. To practice self-harm is to leave behind a record that others cannot ignore.

Jesus could not have told the Samaritan woman everything she ever did if he had never bothered to know her. In her encounter with Jesus she felt known, really known. She felt recognized and valued and affirmed. Above all, she felt loved. In him her search came to an end. In him her deepest desire found satisfaction.

Her witness in her town spreads like a virus. She is so persuasive that the townspeople decide to invite Jesus to stay with them. Jesus consents and begins to speak to them his word. They too arrive at the same conclusion as did the Samaritan woman: "We have heard for ourselves, and we know that this is truly the Savior of the world" (John 4:42).

Can we concur with the townspeople after hearing this word? What does the lesson of the Samaritan woman have to teach us today? We have stressed that in Jesus she found living water, which satisfied her thirst so completely that she will never thirst again. Do we find in Christ this same living water?

If we do not, then, perhaps paradoxically, we have to refuse to let our thirst be quenched. The heart is always thirsty and like a deer pants for flowing waters. But it tends to be drawn to sources that do not deliver on their promise to satisfy. What are *we* looking for to satisfy our deepest longings? Let us not settle for counterfeits, which narrow and even disfigure our lives, preventing us from becoming all that God has called us to be. Instead, let us always look to Christ to satisfy. Let us ask God to pour his love into our hearts so that we have a constant desire for Christ. Then we will be able to say with the Psalmist: "You, O

God, you are my God, earnestly I seek you; I thirst for you, my whole being longs for you, in a dry and parched land where there is no water" (63:1). Then we will remain in him, from whom will flow streams of living waters in the barren deserts of our lives. Amen.

16

A DRAMA OF CONVERSION

JOHN 9:1-41

We have already mentioned that the gospel lessons appointed for this season of Lent present to us portraits of conversion. But these portraits are by no means lifeless or one-dimensional. For this reason, perhaps the expression "dramas of conversion" is the more appropriate one to use. Many Bible students claim that the Gospel of John is the most dramatic book of the New Testament. After an opening chapter in which it proclaims the significance of Jesus for all reality, this Gospel moves into a series of well-crafted scenes. There is action; there is suspense; there are characters who are compelled to interact with each other after the "unexpected" brings them together.

Perhaps nowhere else is there more support for this claim than in this lesson. The cast of characters includes Jesus and his disciples, the man born blind, his parents, and the Pharisees, among others. The action is complex; the dialogue among the characters is subtle and engaging. It's a scene that demands more than one reading. With each re-reading, something new appears that we didn't notice before.

On this occasion, however, we will isolate from our reading a single theme, the theme of conversion. Now conversion in John's Gospel always means a transition from unbelief to belief, from ignorance to knowledge. That dramatizing conversions should be a focus for John makes sense in light of the purpose of his Gospel: "These are written so that you may believe Jesus is the Christ, the Son of God, and that by believing you may have life in his name" (20:31).

What specifically can we learn about conversion from *this* drama? Let me suggest it can be analyzed into three points: First, God is *for* suffering humanity; second, God touches us before and apart from our knowledge of him; and third and finally, God desires us to place our faith in him. Let us then devote the next few moments to considering each of these in turn.

When I was a student shopping one day for textbooks in our seminary's bookstore, I saw one whose title made me pause: *Why, God?* I'm sure we have all asked this question. We ask it especially in times of pain and suffering. "If you are good and all-powerful, why did you let this happen to me?" Since as human beings, we are meaning-making creatures, we're not content to live without an explanation. It's intolerable for us; we must have an answer. That's why we search our past to see whether or not our suffering has its cause there. We assume we must be suffering as we are now because of something we did then.

"Who sinned, this man, or this man's parents, that he has been born blind?" (John 9:2). Note that Jesus does not go down this rabbit hole with his disciples. Instead, he denies the connection between the man's present condition and his past or his parents' past and redirects the disciples' attention to the present.

How do we react to this? Can this be a totally satisfying answer to our question about our suffering? Perhaps we should step back and ask instead: "What gives us more comfort? That God can make sense of our past, or that God continues to work in our present?" "While daylight lasts we must carry on the work of him who sent me," Jesus tells his disciples (John 9:4). The fact is that we may never find a satisfying explanation for the bad things that happened to us. But we can trust God here and now, the God who is working to heal and restore us and all creation, in order to display his power and glory.

This is an important point. Whenever we cannot make sense of our lives, whenever we cannot connect the dots, God gently draws us out of our preoccupation with our past to what he is doing now. Our God is a living God. He does not abandon the world but is present and active within it. Of this God Jesus says: "My Father is always at his work to this very day, and I too am working" (John 5:17). A wise preacher once said: "God does not meet us in our past, so don't go there to look for him; rather, God meets us in the present. Search for God in the here and now." God is still working in and around us.

Now if God is *for* suffering humanity, it stands to reason that he actively searches us out. Note that the man does not seek Jesus out. Rather, Jesus sees him. Jesus decides to act before and apart from the man's request to be healed. We have now arrived at our second point. What Jesus does for this man in response to his suffering is an act of sheer grace. Now let us reflect for a moment on the implications.

All the man knows is what happened to him. He can recall the meeting with Jesus. He can recount what this man did to him, what he instructed him to do, but that is all he really knows. When his neighbors ask him where this man who healed him is, he replies, "I do not know." When the Pharisees ask him about Jesus, he tells them only about what he did for him. When they press him to blaspheme the name of Jesus, again he can only say: "Whether or not he is a sinner, I do not know." Again, all he does know is what Jesus did for him: "Once I was blind, now I can see" (John 9:25).

When God meets us to heal us, to change us, to set our life on a new course, to give us new hope, we don't necessarily know how to name this God, at least not very well, or at least not at first. We do know, however, that we are different. We do know we are no longer who we once were.

What is it that most draws people to consider seriously the claims of the Christian faith? It's what they see in another person. We may know of someone who once lived a morally reckless life. Today, however, he is changed. His problems have not disappeared; by no means is he perfect, but he is no longer who he once was. When he tells us it's because of the God who met him, then we are inclined to listen.

Then there are those who claim to know God. They tell us about this God. They explain to us how God acts in the world. They are sure about those whom God blesses, about those whom God curses. They seem to be knowledgeable, but there is nothing about their lives that makes their talk about God attractive to us.

In this regard, the healed man in our drama appears as a foil to the Pharisees. This man, whom the Pharisees regard of no account, whom they expel from the synagogue, whose sin, they claim, disqualifies him from teaching them truth about God—it is this man who sees. He can tell us something true about God. The Pharisees, on the other hand, who insist they know God's law, who presume to be disciples of Moses, who imagine they can distinguish a true prophet from a false one—it is they who are blind. They can tell us nothing about God.

Of course, the healed man does not yet know as he ought to know. After he heard that the Pharisees expelled him from the synagogue, Jesus finds the man. He asks him directly: "Do you believe in the Son of Man?" (John 9:35). The man has still to come to a knowledge of the God who healed him. Jesus encounters him a first time to heal him; he encounters him a second time to reveal himself to him. This elicits in him faith, which in turn prompts him to worship.

Here we arrive at our third and final point. God desires us to place our faith in him. Let us be clear. God is gracious and compassionate to people regardless of whether they place their faith in him. He does good to them apart from their response. But implied in the question: "Do you believe in the Son of Man?" is the invitation to receive God's gift. "For God so loved the world that he gave his only begotten Son, that whoever believes in him should not perish but have eternal life" (John 3:16). Amen.

17

NO MORE TEARS

JOHN 11:1-45

The gospel lesson designated for this Lord's Day invites us to reflect on tears. Tears, of course, are manifestations of emotions. But tears in themselves do not tell us which emotion they are manifesting. There are tears of joy, as well as tears of relief. There are even tears that flow when people are seized with uncontrollable laughter. But tears are most often a manifestation of sadness. When we think about occasions that bring sadness, there is one that stands out above the rest. We refer here to the death of a loved one. In the gospel lesson a death is recounted. Of course, this death is noteworthy for an obvious reason, as we will examine later. But let not this extraordinary death eclipse from our view that what is recounted here is a death of one loved by Jesus. His name is Lazarus. And he and his two sisters, Mary and Martha, were close friends to Jesus. In fact, John tells us explicitly that Jesus loved them. Now the death of Lazarus affected Jesus just as the death of our loved one affects us: Jesus wept.

That would be insignificant in itself. It is a normal occurrence in a world where each life is surrounded by death. "In the midst of life, we are in death," as the memorable line from the old Gregorian chant expresses it. But in the sentence, "Jesus wept," the stress ought to fall not on the predicate but the subject: It is *Jesus* who wept. Why this is significant will become clear as we proceed in our meditation on this lesson. To this end, we will organize our observations around the verbs that indicate Jesus' emotional state in the face of the death of his friend Lazarus. We will observe first that Jesus is troubled; then we will note that Jesus is deeply moved in spirit.

Jesus is troubled when he enters upon a scene where people are mourning. That is to say, they are crying aloud. Public wailing was a common feature in funeral rites in the ancient world, even in very traditional societies in our world today. Did you ever notice that crying is contagious? Even when they see and hear the tears of actors on the screen in a sad movie, moviegoers will often also be moved to cry themselves. Jesus is troubled when he sees and hears the tears of the people. Their sorrow compounds his own sorrow.

The scene may and should recall for us the Old Testament prophecies: "In all their distress, he too was distressed and the angel of his presence saved them" (Isa. 63:9). "He was a man of sorrows and acquainted with grief" (Isa. 53:3). "Surely he has borne our griefs and carried our sorrows" (Isa. 53:4).

For us this is a source of immense comfort. In times of extreme distress, people tend to complain that God is distant. Even if God is not distant, since he's God and therefore present everywhere, at least it seems difficult during these times to be convinced that really God cares. But what does it even mean to say that God cares?

To be God is to lack nothing. That is to say, to be God is to be self-sufficient. God is himself the source of all he needs to be God, as the theologians tell us. Put otherwise, we may say that God is the source of his own fulfillment, the source of his own happiness. This is implied in the biblical affirmation that God is love. The love of the Father for the Son and the Son for Father in the bond of the Holy Spirit is the source of the perfect contentment and joy and peace and blessedness within which the one God lives and loves as God. It is common for people to imagine that God created the world, the angels and all the people in it, because he was lonely and therefore needed the company. If this is the case, then God created all things out of a sense of lack. But this cannot be, if what we have claimed about God is true. In this sense the life that is God's and the life that is ours cannot be more different or farther removed. But Jesus wept. That is astonishing in light of what the Gospel of John teaches us about Jesus—that he is the incarnate Word of God and therefore is God. It means that in the person of the Son, God really has entered into human experience, that God himself has somehow known lack and undergone loss.

We have to dwell on this for a few moments. Lazarus was one of the few friends of Jesus mentioned by name in the Gospels. We're even told that Jesus loved him, as we have already noted. We have further noted that Jesus responded as would anyone who loses a loved one. He wept. Even some of the Jews present there called attention to this fact. This manifestation of sorrow is a sign of Jesus' love for Lazarus.

It is important to underline here that it's the death of this one man, this one man who has a name, that Jesus mourns. But what is the meaning of the death of a man, of our own death? No doubt there are a wide range of answers. But two seem to be especially prominent. The first is that death is natural or proper to us. We ought to accept it as inevitable. We ought to face it with courage and equanimity. Death is part of the life cycle. It appears as a good in view of generational succession. From dust we came and to dust we return. One generation must pass away to make room for the next. The second view is that death is unnatural. A human death is not merely a death of one member of a species. What it is that dies when a man or woman dies is a person with a unique and irreplaceable identity. This is why we experience loss when a loved one dies. And the loss of this unique person of irreplaceable worth to us causes us sorrow.

Those who sorrow over their loss of a loved one need to know that they are not abandoned to their sorrow. God in Jesus Christ stands in solidarity with them as one of them. In the person of the incarnate Son, God himself has known what it's like to lose a loved one. How is it possible to make this claim? The Christian faith points to the incarnation. It says: "Here is proof that God understands the human pain that comes from the loss of loved one. Here is proof that God can and does know loss and lack. Jesus, the incarnate Word of God and therefore God, lost a loved one to death, and he wept."

But it is not enough to say that God understands, that God is with us in our pain. If that is all that God can do, then he is an impotent God whom it is possible to admire but not to worship as God. That is why we said that only for a few moments can we dwell on the reality that Jesus wept. We cannot stay there. We have to see now how this drama plays out; we have to see what happens next.

Jesus does not stay with the mourners. He inquires about the grave. He wants to know where Lazarus has been laid to rest. They escort him to the grave. It was a cave, and a stone was lying upon it.

Jesus does not walk to the grave without emotion. There is a verb here that indicates Jesus' emotional state. It is one that John has already used in verse 33, where we read that Jesus is "deeply moved." Noteworthy is that this verb is repeated. We read in verse 38 that Jesus was "once more deeply moved." Here the verb expresses an indignation in the face of what God finds most repugnant, most objectionable. We refer here to death. God finds death repugnant because it is God's contrary. God is life. Contraries repel and exclude one another. Death has spoiled God's good creation. Death contradicts God's intention and plan for his people, whom he ordained for fellowship with him in a covenant that is everlasting.

That Jesus is deeply moved expresses his indignation. According to Karl Barth, this emotional state reveals God's resolute "No!" to the reality of death. So Jesus is not only sorrowful and troubled; he is also indignant. He is indignant in the face of death.

But there is more to be seen in this verb. Scholars tell us that in the original it means "to snort like a horse." I don't know what makes a horse snort. I do know, however, that interpreters have suggested that the snort could be that of a war horse ready for battle.

Parenthetically, the loss of our loved one to death does not constitute evidence that God is against us. That claim contradicts what we feel when we lose a loved one. In Ruth we read that after Naomi lost her husband and her two sons in the land of Moab, she concluded that the Lord's hand was against her. When she returned to Bethlehem to try to rebuild her life, she told the townspeople not to call her Naomi but Marah. Marah means bitterness. "Call me Mara, because the Almighty has made my life very bitter. Why call me Naomi? The Lord has afflicted me; the Almighty has brought misfortune upon me" (Ruth 1:20-21). It is common to attribute the personal catastrophes that inevitably overtake us to God. That is, it is natural to blame God. It seems that both Martha and Mary indirectly blame Jesus for the death of her brother: "Lord, if you had been here, my brother would not have died" (John 11:21, 32). How often have we thought or said the same thing! "God, if you had heard and answered my prayer, my loved one would not have died. God, if you had heard and answered my prayer, my dream would not have died."

But Jesus does not stand against men and women in their sadness and sorrow. He fights for them. And at this stage in the drama Jesus prepares to wage war against death. He intrudes upon it and attacks it. Death is called a foe in the Bible. And the last enemy to be destroyed is death, according to the Apostle Paul (1 Cor. 15:26). And death and hell were cast into the lake of fire, according to the seer (Rev. 20:14). When Jesus came to the tomb and to the stone laying upon it, he came to do battle. In his commentary on this text, John Calvin observes that "Christ does not approach the sepulcher as an idle spectator, but as a champion who prepares for a contest; and therefore, we need not wonder that he groans; for the violent tyranny of death, which he had to conquer, is placed before his eyes."

The drama resolves itself with four commands that demonstrate Jesus' charge over the situation: "Take away the stone! Lazarus come out! Unbind him! Let him go!" In these four commands we see Jesus wage his successful battle against his enemy, which is death.

The raising of Lazarus from the dead is the most powerful, the most awe-inspiring miracle recounted in the Gospel of John thus far. That Jesus has absolute power over death John wants to make unmistakably clear. Evidence for our claim here can be found in Martha's objection to Jesus' command to remove the stone. "But Lord, by this time there is a bad odor, for he has been there four days" (John 11:39). Commentators tell us that John includes this detail in recognition of the Jewish belief that a dead person is really dead only after three days. This notion can be extended. The third day is the decisive day, the critical day on which something is definitively concluded. So also with death: After three days it is finally certain whether all hope is to be abandoned.

The emergence of Lazarus from a cave after four days is a sign. And the function of a sign in the Gospel of John is always to confront the reader with the question: "Will you believe that this Jesus is the one he claims to be?" To be more specific in this context: "Will you believe that there is a power greater than that of death, that this power is in Jesus Christ, or that this power is Jesus Christ?"

In this regard, it is instructive to consider the response of Martha to Jesus when he arrives on the scene. The crisis that the women were undergoing in waiting for a delayed Jesus while their brother's condition was becoming more and more critical actually yields to another crisis. It is a now a crisis of faith. "Your brother will rise again," Jesus tells Martha (John 11:23). "I know he will rise again in the resurrection at the last day" she replies in the following verse.

That response in fact represents a helpless resignation to the turn of events over which she now has no control. Behind these words we can hear her say to herself: "My brother is dead. I have no choice but to be a good and faithful and devout Sunday school girl and confess what we all confess." But what is that to her? It does not necessarily touch her where she lives at the moment. It represents something safe for her to retreat behind. But Jesus does not let her retreat behind it. He does not allow her to languish in a state of helpless resignation. Instead he challenges her. "I am the resurrection and the life" (John 11:25). "I am here before you. Will you believe that I am who I claim to be? If you believe, you will see the glory of God."

Let us be clear. The crisis in which she now finds herself in confrontation with Jesus is not the crisis precipitated by a mortally ill brother and a healer who did not arrive on time to do anything about it. It is a crisis of faith.

In the last analysis, is this not what is at issue for us too? The crisis is not whether or not we have a high enough view of the truth of scripture to affirm that Jesus really called a dead man out of a tomb after four days. The crisis is not whether or not we can affirm the articles of the creed suggested by our lesson: "I believe in the resurrection of the body and the life everlasting." Yes! But there are moments for us too, moments when it as just as easy to adopt an attitude of passive resignation to the death that everywhere surrounds us as it was for Martha and Mary. Then these words are nothing more than the prevailing orthodoxy behind which it is just as easy for us to retreat as it was for Martha. Note that the tense in which Jesus declares himself to be resurrection and the life is present. Jesus challenges us just as he did Martha and to the generations of peoples who followed hers even to our own. "I am the resurrection and the life. He who believes in me will live, even though he dies, and whoever lives and believes in me will never die" (John 11:25, 26). Do we believe this?

SUBDUING HIS ENEMIES
MATTHEW 21:1-11

The gospel lesson designated for this Lord's Day, which is Palm Sunday, reveals a longing. There's a longing in the human heart for a strong leader. That probably doesn't seem obvious. Many will say: "Let me earn a living. Let me raise my family. And don't interfere too much." The eighteenth-century playwright Voltaire counseled us to ignore the violence and plunder of kings and mind our own business. He famously said we must take care of our own gardens. It sounds good, but when times are chaotic, when our institutions fail, we long for a strong leader to restore order and to assure us that everything will be fine. That's why those in power are fearful in times of civil unrest. Remember Germany in the 1930s? Closer to home are the demagogues who emerged during the Great Depression. Charles Coughlin, the Catholic priest from Detroit, seized the new medium of radio and stirred up the passions of millions.

In retrospect, we see these figures as dangerous. But their appearance is always a very present possibility in our world. In fact, some are afraid that they'll arise again in our own time, especially if the current public health and social crises escalate. But why are we so drawn to these figures when they do arise? It's because they appeal to our imagination. With their charisma, with their words, they paint us a picture of a better world—a lost Eden where justice prevails and prosperity abounds.

Let us for a moment imagine the world of Jesus. Today, Palm Sunday, he's riding into Jerusalem on a donkey. This is a public action, fraught with meaning. Before, he moved around incognito. He even warned people not to tell others about him. But that's all behind him now. When his disciples seated him on the donkey, when the people spread out their cloaks before him, when the crowds shouted their hosannas, there can be no more uncertainty. This is the last king of Israel, the Son of David, to whom the promises of God apply. This is the heir from David's own body, whose throne God promised to establish forever.

Let's consider the scene more closely. Why does Jesus ride a donkey? It's in keeping with the kings before him. Solomon succeeds his father David as king. He rides David's mule. This is a public proclamation that Solomon's rule is under David's blessing (1 Kings 1:32-40). Later, Jehu is anointed as king by a prophet. When Jehu told others that a prophet anointed him as king, they immediately spread their cloaks before him to acknowledge him as their new monarch (2 Kings 9:12, 13). If this is still unclear, later prophecy spells it out: "Tell the daughter of Zion, look, your king is coming to you, humble, and mounted on a donkey, and on a colt, the foal of a donkey" (Zech. 9:9). When the Jews see Jesus on the donkey, they will understand what's going on. This is the Davidic king they have been expecting for hundreds of years.

As the people responded to Jehu with a shout, "Hail, King of the Jews!" so now they cry out today: "Hosanna, to the Son of David!" "Hosanna" means "save us now!" It is addressed to the one through whom God's saving power flows—in acts of love, healing, and forgiveness. Now Jesus enters into Jerusalem, the city of the great king. He's about to assume his rightful throne. Jesus' reign as king will bring heaven's peace to earth. This is the climactic moment! "Hosanna in the highest!"—the people's praise echoes that of the angels on that first Christmas night. "Glory to God in the highest! Peace on earth and good will towards all" (Luke 2:14). Could this really be happening?

We know how widespread the hope was in those days, not only among the Jews but also among the Romans. Public documents that date back to the time of the emperor Augustus make this clear. With his rise to power, the people hailed him as Savior. They celebrated him as a god whose birth signaled that a new age was dawning. With him the bloody civil wars ended; with him a universal reign of peace was about to begin. The words from an inscription found at Halicarnassus puts this eloquently:

> *For pacified is the earth and the sea; the cities flourish, there is love of order, concord, good fellowship, prosperity, and abundance of everything good. With hopes for the future, and good feeling toward the present, mankind is fulfilled.*

These are the kind of words that conjure up for us an image of our lost Eden.

But did Augustus Caesar and his successors live up to these hopes? Listen to the Roman historian Tacitus, writing a mere 85 years after the death of Augustus.

> *To ravage, to slaughter, to usurp under false titles, the Romans call empire; and where they make a desert, they call it peace.*

Indeed, to make peace, or pacification, came to mean something entirely different. It means to subdue your enemies by force. Imposing peace by violence—that is a contradiction in terms. But that was and is our world. No restoration of Eden here; only disappointed hopes.

But what about Jesus? It's interesting to read the rest of the prophecy in Zechariah, even though Matthew's Gospel does not include it. "He will cut off the chariot from Israel and the war-horse from Jerusalem, and the battle bow shall be cut off, and he shall command peace to the nations" (Zech. 9:10). This king, riding on a colt, will banish war from the land—no more chariots, war horses, or bows. Commanding peace to the nations, he will be the king of peace.

The same hopes are invested in him. But what happened? That will unfold in the upcoming days. We know there will be a fatal collision. He has enemies who reject his claim to be king. One of his disciples hands him over to his enemies. Finally, the Jewish authorities arrest him, try him, and hand him over to the Romans. They condemn him to a violent death.

Violence predominated then, as it still does today. Rulers still use violence to protect their power. And revolutionaries still use violence to seize power. But Jesus will not play be these rules. He will not impose peace by violence. That is a contradiction in terms. He will absorb it in his own body on the cross. It's on the cross that he subdues his enemies, making them friends of God and of each other. It's on the cross that he will be revealed as king of peace. But about this we will learn more later this week.

We celebrate on Palm Sunday. The mood is festive. From the time it was adopted by the church in the middle ages, the procession with palms has had a triumphal character. It was a real feast of Christ the King. So let us observe Palm Sunday with joy.

At the same time, let us not miss the meaning of those acclamations. We have already said that "Hosanna!" means "save us now." How many people in our world are still crying out today: "O Lord, save us now! Save us from pestilence and violence and death!"

The Christian faith is an "already/not yet faith." God's people have already been saved, but saved in hope (Rom. 8:24). God's people already have the "guarantee of the Spirit" (Eph. 1:13-14), but they don't yet have the "glorious freedom of the children of God" (Rom. 8:21). Christ has already been enthroned as king, but his kingdom has not yet come on earth, as it is in heaven.

Today we are undergoing a global crisis. The social and economic costs will probably be high. There may be profound civil unrest. Leaders will emerge. Don't place your ultimate hope in them. They can't save us. And if the crisis worsens and demagogues emerge, don't even listen to them. They can destroy us.

Instead, place your hope in the resurrected and ascended Christ, the prince of peace, the king of kings and lord of lords. Shelter in place in him. He is a wise and benevolent king. He is faithful to watch over us and provide for us. He is in control. And one day this will be manifest to all. Amen.

CPSIA information can be obtained
at www.ICGtesting.com
Printed in the USA
LVHW050758060121
675395LV00006B/684